GREAT ISLAMIC THINKERS

Al-Fārābi, Founder of Islamic Neoplatonism

His Life, Works and Influence

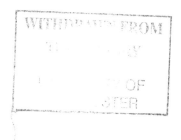

RELATED TITLES PUBLISHED BY ONEWORLD

Muslim Women Mystics: The Life of Rabi'a and Other Women Mystics in Islam, Margaret Smith, ISBN 1–85168–250–3

Faith and Reason in Islam: Averroes' Exposition of Religious Arguments, edited and translated by Ibrahim Najjar, ISBN 1–85168–263–5

Averroes: His Life, Works and Influence, Majid Fakhry, ISBN 1–85168–269–4

Rumi – Past and Present, East and West: The Life, Teachings and Poetry of Jalâl al-Din Rumi, Franklin D. Lewis, ISBN 1–85168–214–7

GREAT ISLAMIC THINKERS

Al-Fārābi, Founder of Islamic Neoplatonism

His Life, Works and Influence

MAJID FAKHRY

ONEWORLD
OXFORD

AL-FĀRĀBI, FOUNDER OF ISLAMIC NEOPLATONISM:
HIS LIFE, WORKS AND INFLUENCE

Oneworld Publications
(Sales and Editorial)
185 Banbury Road
Oxford OX2 7AR
England
www.oneworld-publications.com

A CIP record for this title is available
from the British Library

ISBN 1-85168-302-X

Cover design by Design Deluxe
Cover picture: School at Aleppo, Syria, Arab Manuscript by Maqamat
d Al Hariri, © the art archive/Bibliothèque nationale de Paris/Josse.
Typeset by LaserScript Ltd, Mitcham, UK
Printed and bound by Bell & Bain Ltd, Glasgow

Contents

Preface

It is generally acknowledged that the first genuine Muslim philosopher was Abū Ya'qūb al-Kindi (d. *c.* 866), whose learning was very vast, as illustrated by his writings on almost all the sciences known in his day, ranging from astronomy to psychology, physics and metaphysics. However, judging from the few writings of this *Arab* philosopher to have survived, al-Kindi tended to be eclectical and rhapsodic in the discussion of his principal themes. The first systematic philosopher in Islam was Abū Naṣr al-Fārābi (d. 950), to whom this volume is devoted. He developed an elaborate emanationist scheme, affiliated to the metaphysics and cosmology of Plotinus (d. 270) and Proclus (d. 450), known as Neoplatonism, which had no precedent in the world of Islam. In addition, he wrote the first Muslim political treatise, inspired by Plato's *Republic* and known as the *Opinions of the Inhabitants of the Virtuous City*. He was also the first outstanding logician of Islam, and paraphrased or commented on the whole Aristotelian logical corpus, known as the *Organon.*

Despite this significant contribution to the history of philosophy and logic, al-Fārābi has received very little attention in the West. M. Steinschneider published in 1889 the first monograph on al-Fārābi, and F. Dieterici published in the next year a collection of his writings accompanied with a German translation. In 1934, Ibrahim Madkour published his *La Place d'al-Fārābi dans l'école philosophique Arabe.* All of these valuable works, however, antedate the discovery and publication of many of al-Fārābi's works, especially in the field of logic. In that area, the editions and translations of M. Mahdi and D.M. Dunlop are particularly noteworthy.

I have tried in the present volume to give a comprehensive account of al-Fārābi's contribution to logic, political theory, metaphysics and music, while highlighting his role as a major link in the transmission of Greek philosophy to the Arabs and his impact on subsequent philosophers, in both the Muslim world and the Latin West. The bibliography at the end of the book will reveal the vast scope of al-Fārābi's contribution and his influence.

Majid Fakhry

Introduction

Abū Naṣr al-Fārābi (870–950), generally referred to in the Arabic sources as the Second Teacher (*al-Mu'allim al-Thāni*), occupies a unique position in the history of philosophy, as the link between Greek philosophy and Islamic thought. His standing in the history of Aristotelian logic is pivotal; no logician of any significance arose anywhere during the period separating Boethius (d. 525), the Roman consul, who translated Aristotle's logical works into Latin, and Abélard (d. 1141) in Western Europe. Of the Arab philosophers who preceded al-Fārābi, al-Kindi (d. *c.* 866), a great champion of Greek philosophy, which was in perfect harmony with Islam, according to him, does not appear to have made a significant contribution to logic, although in other respects his learning was vast. Al-Rāzi (d. *c.* 925) had the highest regard for the Greeks, and in particular for Plato, 'the master and leader of all the philosophers', but regarded philosophy and religion as incompatible. As the greatest non-conformist in Islam, he rejected the whole fabric of revelation and substituted for the official Islamic view five co-eternal principles, the Creator (*Bāri'*), the soul, matter, space and time, inspired in part by Plato and the Harranians.

It will be shown in due course how al-Fārābi, in a lost treatise on the *Rise of Philosophy*, traced the history of Greek philosophy from the time of Aristotle, as it passed through the Alexandrian medium, during the Ptolemaic period, down to the Islamic period and up to his own time.

In some of his other writings, he expounded the philosophies of Aristotle and Plato in some detail and gave a succinct account of the Presocratics. His own teacher in logic, Yuḥanna Ibn Ḥaylān, as well as the leading logicians of the time, Abū Bishr Matta (d. 940), the Bishop, Isrā'il Quwayri, and Ibrahim al-Marwazi, are mentioned in the *Rise of Philosophy*, given in the Appendix. However, none of those Syriac logicians had gone beyond the first four books of Aristotelian logic, the *Isagoge* of Porphyry, the *Categories*, *De Interpretatione* and the first parts of *Analytica Priora*, because of the threat to Christian religious belief that the study of the other parts, especially the *Analytica Posteriora*, known in Arabic as the *Book of Demonstration* (*Kitāb al-Burhān*), was thought to present. Al-Fārābi was in that respect the first logician to break with the Syriac tradition; his logical commentaries and paraphrases covered the whole range of Aristotelian logic, to which, following the Syriac tradition, the *Rhetorica* and *Poetica* were added, as we will see in due course.

Not only in the sphere of logic, but also in cosmology and metaphysics, al-Fārābi stands out as a leading figure. Neither al-Kindi nor al-Rāzi had contributed substantially to the systematization of cosmology and metaphysics. Al-Fārābi should be regarded, therefore, as the first system-builder in the history of Arab-Islamic thought. He built upon Plotinus's emanationist scheme a cosmological and metaphysical system that is striking for its intricacy and daring. Thoroughly imbued with the Neoplatonic spirit of that Greek-Egyptian philosopher, mistakenly identified with Aristotle in the Arabic sources, al-Fārābi developed in his principal writings, such as the *Virtuous City* (*al-Madīnah al-Fāḍilah*) and the *Civil Polity* (*al-Siyāsah al-Madaniyah*) an elaborate metaphysical scheme in which the Qur'ānic concepts of creation, God's sovereignty in the world and the fate of the soul after death are interpreted in an entirely new spirit. This scheme is then artfully coupled with a political scheme, reminiscent of Plato's utopian model in the *Republic*.

In the metaphysical scheme, God or the First Being (*al-Awwal*), as al-Fārābi prefers to call Him, following the example of Proclus of Athens (d. 485), the last great Greek expositor of Neoplatonism, stands at the apex of the cosmic order; but unlike the One (*Tô hen*) of Plotinus (d. 270) or the First (*Tô Prôton*) of Proclus, who are above being and thought, al-Fārābi's God is identical with Aristotle's Unmoved Mover, who is thought thinking itself (*'aql*, *'āqil* and *ma'qūl*) and the Being from whom all other beings emanate. From this First Being, through a process of progressive emanation or overflowing (*fayḍ* or *ṣudūr*) arise the successive orders of intellect (*'aql*), soul (*nafs*) and prime matter (*hayūla*). Once it has fulfilled its destiny as a citizen of the higher or intelligible world, the soul is able, through conjunction (*ittiṣāl*) with the last of the intellects, known as the Active Intellect, to rejoin its original abode in that higher world.

The emanationist concept, despite its patent similarity to the Qur'ānic concept of creation (*khalq*, *ibdā'*), so graphically expressed in the Qur'ān in terms of God's omnipotence and omniscience, is vastly removed from it. No wonder this issue became in time the focus of the most heated controversies between the Islamic philosophers and the theologians (*Mutakallimūn*), best illustrated in the onslaught of al-Ghazāli (d. 1111) on the two chief expositors of Neoplatonism in Islam, al-Fārābi and Ibn Sīna (d. 1037). The form that controversy took was whether the concept of the world as an eternal or everlasting emanation from God was reconcilable with the Islamic doctrine according to which the world is created in time and *ex nihilo* (*ḥadith*, *muḥdath*) by a divine act of peremptory command (*amr*).

As regards the soul (*nafs*), the controversy turned on whether the human soul is simply a fragment of the universal soul, which moves the heavenly spheres, and through the Active Intellect the terrestrial order below, or a creation of God destined to survive the destruction of the body, to which it will be reunited miraculously in the Hereafter.

According to the Islamic Neoplatonic scheme, which al-Fārābi was the first to develop, the series of intellects (*'uqūl*) and souls (*nufūs*) terminates in the emergence of the terrestrial realm, which consists of those animate and inanimate entities referred to collectively as the world of generation and corruption. This scheme, which is of undoubted Neoplatonic origin, is attributed to Aristotle on account of a strange literary accident; namely, the fact that the translation of the last three books of Plotinus's *Enneads* were mistakenly attributed to Aristotle and circulated accordingly under the rubric of *Ātulugia Arisṭutālīs* (*The Theology of Aristotle*), or the *Book of Divinity*.

As a counterpart to the above-mentioned cosmological scheme, al-Fārābi conceived of humankind, by reason of their rational nature, as a link between the intelligible world and the lower material world of generation and corruption. Endowed with a series of faculties – the nutritive, the perceptual, the imaginative and the rational – humans are unable to achieve their ultimate goal of happiness or well-being (*sa'ādah*) without the assistance of their fellows. This is how political association (*ijtimā'*) in the form of large, intermediate and small communities, identified by al-Fārābi with the inhabited world (*ma'mūrah*), the nation and the city, arises.

Here al-Fārābi draws a close parallel between the state and the body, whose parts or organs form a hierarchy of members assisting each other, led by a ruling member who in the case of the state is the chief ruler (*ra'īs*) and in the case of the body is the heart. This theme is developed in some detail but also with some repetitiveness in al-Fārābi's principal political treatises, including the *Virtuous City* (*al-Madīnah al-Fāḍilah*), the *Civil Polity* (*al-Siyāsah al-Madaniyah*) and the *Attainment of Happiness* (*Tahsīl al-Sa'ādah*), in a manner that illustrates his pre-eminence as the chief political philosopher of Islam. It is more accurate, perhaps, to designate him as the founder of Islamic political philosophy, on whom all writers on this subject, such as Ibn Bājjah (d. 1138) and Naṣir al-Din al-Ṭūsi (d. 1274) actually depended.

Of al-Fārābi's immediate successors, Ibn Sīna (d. 1037) was his immediate spiritual disciple and successor. Committed essentially to the same Neoplatonic view of reality, Ibn Sīna was able to develop on the basis of al-Fārābi's emanationist scheme a much more systematic view of the cosmic hierarchy and especially humankind's progression from the lower disposition to know, called by him the passive or material intellect, to that 'conjunction' with the Active Intellect in which all human intellectual aspirations are fulfilled. When someone achieves this condition, argues Ibn Sīna, their soul becomes a replica of the intelligible world, of which it was a denizen prior to its descent into the human body.

Despite their agreement on the fundamental principles of Neoplatonism, it is noteworthy that Ibn Sīna's style of writing is more discursive or thematic and is reminiscent of Aristotle's 'treatise' style. Al-Fārābi's style by contrast tends to be rhapsodic and is reminiscent of Plato's style in the *Dialogues*.

However, in substantive terms, Ibn Sīna's contributions to ethics and politics, which loom so large in al-Fārābi's work, were rather negligible. Unlike Ibn Sīna, al-Fārābi's thought was dominated by ethical and political concerns and a dedication to the search for happiness, with its two components of knowledge (*'ilm*) and virtue.

Al-Fārābi's other disciples or successors in the East included Yahia Ibn 'Adi (d. 974), Miskawayh (d. 1037) and the above-mentioned Nasīr al-Din al-Ṭūsi, and in the West, Ibn Bājjah, his greatest spiritual disciple and commentator in the fields of political philosophy and logic, as we will see in due course.

It is to be noted that despite his standing as the first system-builder in the history of Islamic philosophy and an outstanding pioneer in the fields of logic and political philosophy, al-Fārābi has received very little attention in our time. The earliest study in a European language was M. Steinschneider's *Al-Fārābi's Leben und Schriften*, which was published in 1889, and was followed in 1934 by I. Madkour's *La Place d'al-Fārābi dans l'école philosophique Musulmane*. Ian R. Netton published in 1992 a short study entitled *Al-Fārābi and His School*, to which should be added articles in English or other Western languages by R. Walzer, M. Mahdi and F. Najjar, which are listed in the Bibliography. Regrettably, the late I. Madkour in his masterly work on Aristotelian logic in the Arabic tradition, published in 1934, has accorded al-Fārābi no more than a passing mention, due to the fact that 'of his many logical works and commentaries on the different parts of the *Organon*, only insufficient fragmentary elements have survived', as he rightly tells us.[1] However, that picture has changed radically in recent years as a number of al-Fārābi's logical works and commentaries have been edited or translated, as the Bibliography at the end of the book shows.

1. *L'Organon d'Aristotle au Monde Arabe*, p. 9.

1

Life and Works

The Arab biographers are unanimous in lavishing on al-Fārābi the highest praise. His full name is given in the Arabic sources as Muhammad Ibn Muhammad Ibn Ūzalāgh Ibn Tarkhān and he is said to have been a native of Fārāb in Transoxiana and of Turkish or Turkoman origin. The earliest biographer, Ṣā'id Ibn Ṣā'id al-Andalusi (d. 1070), speaks eloquently of al-Fārābi's contribution to logic. Having studied logic with Yuḥanna Ibn Ḥaylān, we are told, he soon 'outstripped all the Muslims in that field ... He explained the obscure parts (of that science) and revealed its secrets ... in books which were sound in expression and intimation, drawing attention to what al-Kindi and others had overlooked in the field of analysis and the methods of instruction.'[1] He is then commended for writing an 'unparalleled treatise' on *The Enumeration of the Sciences* (*Iḥṣā' al-'Ulūm*) and an equally masterly treatise on the *Philosophy of Plato and Aristotle*, on metaphysics and politics, the *Civil Polity* (*al-Siyāsah al-Madaniyah*) and the *Virtuous Regime* (*al-Sīrah al-Fāḍilah*), as this biographer calls al-Fārābi's best-known treatise, *The Virtuous City* (*al-Madīnah al-Fāḍilah*). These treatises, according to Sā'id, embody the fundamental principles of Aristotle's philosophy, bearing on the 'six spiritual principles and the way in which corporeal substances derive from them',[2] a clear

1. *Tabaqāt al-Umam*, p. 53. Cf. al-Qifti, *Tārikh al-Hukamā'*, p. 277.
2. Ibid., p. 54. Cf. al-Qifti, *Tārikh al-Hukamā'*, p. 278.

reference to the emanationist scheme of Plotinus (d. 270), confused with Aristotle in the Arabic sources, as we saw in the Introduction.

This information is supplemented in later sources by references to al-Fārābi coming to Damascus, where he worked as a garden-keeper; then he moved to Baghdad, where he devoted himself to the study of the Arabic language, which he did not know, although, we are told, he was conversant with Turkish as well as many other languages.[3]

In Baghdad, he soon came into contact with the leading logician of his day, Abū Bishr Matta (d. 911) and a less-known logician, Yuḥanna Ibn Ḥaylān, with whom he studied logic, as we are told in his lost tract, *On the Rise of Philosophy.* Apart from his travels to Egypt and Ascalon, the most memorable event in his life was his association with Sayf al-Dawlah (d. 967), the Hamdāni ruler of Aleppo, a great patron of the arts and letters. Sayf al-Dawlah appears to have had the highest regard for this philosopher of frugal habits and ascetic demeanor, who distinguished himself in a variety of ways, not least of which was music. Apart from the large *Musical Treatise* (*Kitāb al-Musiqa al-Kabīr*), coupled with treatises on *Melody* (*Fi'l Īqā'*) and *Transition to Melody* (*al-Nuqlah ilā'l-Īqā'*) and a small musical tract, al-Fārābi is reported to have been a skillful musician. Once, we are told, he played so skillfully in the presence of Sayf al-Dawlah that his audience was moved to tears; but when he changed his tune, they laughed and finally they fell asleep, whereupon, we are told, he got up and walked away unnoticed.[4] Following his visit to Egypt in 949, he returned to Damascus, where he died in 950.[5]

His lost tract, the *Rise of Philosophy*, contains additional autobiographical information. After reviewing the stages through which Greek philosophy passed from the Classical to the Alexandrian periods, he describes how instruction in logic moved from Alexandria to Baghdad, where Ibrahim al-Marwazi, Abū Bishr Matta and Yūḥanna Ibn Ḥaylān were the most distinguished teachers. Instruction in logic had been confined hitherto, we are told, to the 'end of the existential moods' on account of the threat the more advanced study of logic presented to the

3. Ibn Abī Usaybi'ah, *'Uyūn al-Anbā'*, p. 606; Ibn Khillikān, *Wafayāt al-A'yān*, IV, p. 239.
4. Ibn Khillikān, *Wafayāt al-A'yān*, IV, p. 242.
5. Ibn Abī Usaybi'ah, *'Uyūn al-Anbā'*, p. 603.

Christian faith. Al-Fārābi appears from that account to have been the first to break with that logical tradition and to proceed beyond the first parts of the *Organon* to the study of *Analytica Posteriora* (*Kitāb al-Burhān*).[6] The study of Aristotelian logic had actually been confined in Nestorian and Jacobite seminaries in Syria and Iraq to the first four treatises of that logic; namely, the *Isagoge* of Porphyry, the *Categories*, on *Interpretation* (*Peri Hermeneias*) and the *Analytica Priora*, known in the Arabic sources as *Kitāb al-Qiyās*.[7]

Be this as it may, the testimony of his biographers is conclusive in highlighting al-Fārābi's role as the first great logician, who soon outstripped both his Muslim predecessors and his Christian contemporaries, such as the above-mentioned Yūḥanna Ibn Ḥaylān and Abū Bishr Matta, his own teachers in logic.

This testimony is confirmed by al-Fārābi's vast logical output, enough of which has survived to justify the high regard in which he was held by the ancients. This output includes a series of large commentaries (*shurūh*) on *Analytica Posteriora*, *Analytica Priora*, the *Categories*, *Isagoge*, *Rhetorica* and *On Interpretation* (*Sharh Kitāb al-'Ibarah*), the only such commentary to have survived.[8] To this list should be added paraphrases of *Analytica Posteriora*, *Analytica Priora*, *Topica*, *Isagoge* and *Sophistica*, as well as a tract on the *Conditions of Certainty* (*Sharā'it al-Yaqīn*).[9] However, his most original logical writings consist of a series of analytical treatises intended to serve as a propaedeuntic to the study of logic, which with the exception of Porphyry's *Isagoge*, or introduction to the *Categories*, had no parallels in ancient or medieval history. They include an *Introductory Treatise* (*Risālah fi'l-Tawṭi'ah*), the *Five Sections* (*al-Fusūl al-Khamsah*), *Terms Used in Logic* (*al-Alfāz al-Musta'malāh fi'l-Manṭiq*) and the *Book of Letters* (*Kitāb al-Hurūf*), all of which have survived and will be discussed in Chapter 4.

Al-Fārābi's physical and meteorological writings include commentaries on the *Physics* (*al-Samā' al-Ṭabi'ī*), as that book was known in Arabic, a treatise on *Changing Entities* (*Fi'l-Mawjūdāt al-Mutaghayrah*), the *Heavens and the World* (*al-Samā' wa'l-'Ālam*), the *Meteorology* (*al-Āthār al-'Ulawiyah*), as

6. Ibid., p. 604. Cf. Appendix at the end of this book.
7. Cf. N. Rescher, 'Al-Farabi on Logical Tradition', pp. 127ff.
8. See Bibliography.
9. See Bibliography.

well as a treatise on the *Perpetuity of Motion* and the *Essence of the Soul* (*Fī Māhiyat al-Nafs*). To these works should be added works on alchemy and astrology, the most important of which is his treatise *On Valid and Invalid Astrological Inferences* (*Fi mā Yaṣuḥ wa lā Yaṣuḥ min 'Ilm Ahkām al-Nujūm*), which has survived. He is also reported to have written a commentary on *al-Majasti*, as Ptolemy's *Almagest* was called in Arabic.

Al-Fārābi's metaphysical and methodological works include a *Treatise on Metaphysics* (*Fi'l-'Ilm al-Ilāhi*), a treatise on the *Harmony of the Opinions of Plato and Aristotle* (*Fī'i Ittifāq Arā' Aflātun wa Aristutālis*, also known as *al-Jam 'Bayn Ra'yay al-Hakīmayn*), a treatise on the *Name of Philosophy (Fī Ism al-Falsafah)*, another on *Philosophy and Its Genesis* (*Fi'l-Falsafah wa Sabab Zubūriha*) and finally the *Enumeration of the Sciences* (*Iḥṣā' al-'Ulūm*).[10]

In the fields of ethics and politics in which al-Fārābi excelled, a number of treatises are given in the ancient sources. The list opens with the *Opinions of the Inhabitants of the Virtuous City* (*Arā' Ahl al-Madīnah al-Fāḍilah*) and the *Civil Polity* (*al-Siyāsah al-Madaniyah*), and includes an *Epitome of Plato's Laws* (*Kitāb al-Nawāmīs*), *Select Sections* (on politics) (*Fusūl Murtaza'ah ... min Aqāwīl al-Qudamā'*), a treatise on the *Attainment of Happiness* (*Taḥsīl al-Sa'ādah*) and a shorter tract entitled *Admonition to Seek the Path of Happiness* (*al-Tanbīh 'alā Sabīl al-Sa'ādah*). To these extant works should be added a commentary on the *Opening Parts of Aristotle's Ethics* (*Sharh Ṣadr Kitāb al-Akhlāq li-'Arisṭuṭālīs*), which is lost.

Finally, as already mentioned, al-Fārābi excelled in the theory and practice of music. His best-known work, entitled the *Large Music* (*Kitāb al-Musiqa al-Kabīr*), has survived; but he is also reported to have written shorter treatises on *Melody* (*Fi'l-Īqā'*) and *Transition to Melody* (*al-Nuqlah ila'l-Īqā'*) and *A Short Discourse on Melody* (*Kalām fi'l-Īqā' Mukhtasar*),[11] which is no longer extant, and to which reference has already been made.

10. See Bibliography.
11. Ibn Abī Usaybi'ah, *'Uyūn al-Anbā'*, p. 608.

2

Al-Fārābi and the Greek Legacy

The genesis of philosophy

As already mentioned, in a lost treatise entitled *On the Rise of Philosophy* (*Fī Zuhūr al-Falsafah*), of which a fragment has survived, al-Fārābi gives us a succinct account of the stages through which philosophy passed and his own position in the chain of philosophers, Greek, Hellenistic, Syriac and Muslim. In that fragment preserved by the thirteenth-century historian Ibn Abi Uṣaybi'ah (d. 1270), al-Fārābi is reported to have written that philosophy flourished during the reign of the Greek kings (i.e. the Classical period), was transmitted to Alexandria following the death of Aristotle (d. 322 BCE) and continued up to the death of Cleopatra (literally: the woman) in 30 BCE During the Ptolemaic period (literally: the reign of the thirteen kings), there arose twelve teachers of philosophy, one of whom was Andronicus (of Rhodes) (d. 40 BCE). Al-Fārābi then credits Augustus the Roman Emperor with the meritorious literary task of inspecting the libraries of Alexandria, where copies of Aristotle's works, going back to the time of Theophrastus (who was Aristotle's immediate successor as head of the Lyceum in Athens (322–288 BCE), had survived. Augustus then ordered these books to be copied and to serve as the basis of instruction to the exclusion of all others. Andronicus was charged with preparing copies of these books, some of which the Emperor carried with him to Rome, the rest being kept in the 'center of instruction' at Alexandria. This Andronicus was also ordered to appoint a successor in Alexandria, so that he himself could accompany the Emperor to Rome. Thus, instruction continued at these two sites until the rise of Christianity; whereupon instruction ceased in Rome but continued in Alexandria.[1]

During the Christian period, we are then told by al-Fārābi, a council of Christian bishops was convened so as to decide which part of that instruction (*ta'līm*) should be kept and which should be dropped. The bishops determined that, of the logical works (of Aristotle), the parts that terminate with the 'existential moods (of the syllogism)' should be taught; including: the *Categories*, *On Interpretation* (*Perihermeneias*, as it was called in Greek and *Fāri Hermenias* in Arabic), the first part of the *Analytica Priora*, and the *Isagoge* of Porphyry. This was actually the practice in the Nestorian and Jacobite seminaries of Harrān, Edessa, Qinnesin and Antioch. The rest of these works of logic – namely, *Analytica Posteriora*, known in the Arabic sources as *Kitāb al-Burhān*, the *Topica* and the *Sophistica* – were to be dropped because they constituted a threat to Christianity.[2]

With the advent of Islam, we are then told, instruction moved from Alexandria to Antioch, where it lasted for a long time. This stage ended when the last teacher of the School of Antioch, whom al-Fārābi does not mention by name, had two students, one from Harrān, the other from Merw. The teacher from Merw had two students, who are given as Ibrāhim al-Marwazi and Yūḥanna Ibn Ḥaylān. The Harrānian teacher, on the other hand, had two students; namely, Isrā'il the Bishop (al-Usquf) and Quwayri. The two students from Merw are then credited with continuing the logical tradition in Baghdad. Thus, Ibrāhim al-Marwazi became the teacher of Mattā Ibn Yunis (or Yunān) (d. 911), while Yūḥanna Ibn Ḥaylān became the teacher of al-Fārābi, as he actually tells us. Al-Fārābi then states explicitly that he studied logic with this Yūḥanna up to the end of *Analytica Posteriora* (*Kitāb al-Burhān*), breaking thus with the Syriac tradition already mentioned.[3]

1. Ibn Abī Uṣaybi'ah, *'Uyūn al-Anbā'*, p. 604. Cf. Appendix.
2. Ibid., p. 225. Cf. N. Rescher, *The Development of Arabic Logic*, p. 19, and Wright, *History of Syriac Literature*, pp. 61f.
3. Ibn Abī Uṣaybi'ah, *'Uyūn al-Anbā'*, p. 605. Cf. Appendix.

Philosophy and religion

Apart from this telescopic account of the rise of philosophy, as reported by Ibn Abī Usaybi'ah, al-Fārābi has given us in some of his extant works his own reflections on the development of the philosophical sciences from the earliest times. Thus, in the *Book of Letters* (*Kitāb al-Ḥurūf*), he begins by observing that genuine or demonstrative (*burhāniyah*) philosophy was preceded in time by dialectical, sophistical and other modes of false logical discourse. In point of time, he observes, the rise of religion (*millah*), 'humanly speaking', is subsequent to the rise of philosophy. Its methods of discourse differ from those of philosophy insofar as it seeks to replace philosophy's theoretical concepts with purely 'imaginative representations', more readily accessible to the public, which it then supports by recourse to dialectical, rather than demonstrative arguments. In fact, the methods used by the 'art of theology' (*Ṣina'āt al-Kalām*), which is subservient to religion, are essentially persuasive (*iqnā'iyah*) and belong to the category of rhetorical arguments, which are even inferior to the dialectical (*jadaliyah*), according to his own tabulation. The function of the theologian, in fact, consists in supporting religion's maxims, by recourse to dialectical and rhetorical arguments, in which imaginative representations tend to replace demonstrative proofs.[4] His arguments, in fact, rest on generally accepted premises, rather than self-evident principles, and he is for that reason regarded by the religious community as a member of the élite (*khāṣṣah*); a possible reference to the office of Imam, especially in Shi'ite usage. For al-Fārābi, however, the philosopher should be regarded as a member of the élite in an absolute sense.

Another discipline that is subservient to religion is jurisprudence (*fiqh*), which has a certain similarity to rational discourse, insofar as its adept seeks to found sound opinions, in practical matters, upon principles or precepts received from the lawgiver (i.e. the Prophet). For that reason, the jurist (*faqīh*) is also assigned by the religious community to the class of the élite, in very much the same way as the physician, as practitioner of the art of healing, which is distinct from the theoretical art of physics, is assigned to that pre-eminent class. However, the order of pre-eminence in

4. *Kitāb al-Ḥurūf*, pp. 131f; cf *Kitāb al-Millah*, p. 48.

which those groups should be placed, according to al-Fārābi, absolutely speaking, is first the philosophers, followed by the dialecticians (*jadaliyyūn*), the sophists, the lawgivers, the theologians and finally the jurists.[5]

The progression from the rhetorical and sophistical methods, used originally in the practical arts, to the philosophical is then described by al-Fārābi as the product of the 'natural yearning of the soul to know the causes of sensible matters on earth, in it or around it, together with what is observed or appears of the heavens'.[6] Thus arises the class of searchers for the causes of these matters in the sciences of mathematics and physics, by recourse to rhetorical and sophistical methods, followed by dialectical methods, until such time as the inadequacy of these methods is revealed. Thereupon, the search for sound or apodeictic (*yaqīni*) methods of instruction starts. These methods include the mathematical and the political, which is a combination of both the dialectical and apodeictic methods, verging on the scientific. This continued to be the case until the time of Plato. The process of scientific investigation, however, reached its zenith only in the days of Aristotle, who clearly distinguished the various methods of instruction. The demonstrative methods were then used in private instruction; whereas dialectical, rhetorical and practical methods were used in public instruction. At this point, the need for political legislation arose as a means of instructing the public by recourse to demonstrative methods in theoretical matters, and general rational methods in practical matters. The art of lawmaking, a prerogative of the prophets, required, according to al-Fārābi, a superior gift of representing 'theoretical intelligibles', as well as 'civil activities' in concrete or imaginative ways, as a means of attaining happiness. This required, in addition, the power of effective persuasion in matters both theoretical and practical. When the laws in both these spheres were promulgated, coupled with the knowledge of the means of teaching the public, religion arose as a means of giving guidance to the public in its search for happiness.[7]

5. Ibid., p. 134.
6. Ibid., p. 150.
7. Ibid., p. 152.

Sometimes, al-Fārābi observes, religion is found to conflict with philosophy, because its adepts are unaware of the fact that religious principles are mere representations (*mithālāt*) of rational concepts proposed by the philosophers. When this happens, the theologians (*ahl al-Kalām*) proceed to rebut the false arguments used by their opponents, by recourse to rhetorical arguments – a clear reference to the role that the Mutakallimun, especially the Mu'tazilites, actually played in rebutting the arguments of Manichean and other enemies of Islam. The double role of *Kalām* is specifically stated in the *Enumeration of the Sciences* (*Iḥṣā' al-'Ulūm*) to consist in supporting sound opinions and virtuous actions laid down by the lawgiver (i.e. the Prophet), and the repudiation of all contrary propositions.[8]

In further discussing the relation of philosophy to religion, al-Fārābi reaffirms the pre-eminence of the former and argues that, to the extent a given religion is farther from philosophy, the farther it is from truth. The problem is compounded when a lawgiver (i.e. a prophet), instead of deriving the opinions or beliefs he intends to teach the public from that philosophical system which happens to exist in his day, actually derives them instead from opinions or beliefs proposed by a preceding religion. The error is further compounded when succeeding lawgivers repeat the same process of following in the footsteps of their religious predecessors.

Sometimes certain religions, which are grounded in the genuine philosophy, are transmitted to certain nations or communities (i.e. *Umam*) whose members are not aware of the fact that the principles or doctrines taught by their religion are simply 'representations' of philosophical principles or maxims, of which they have no knowledge. Thereupon, animosity between philosophy and religion mounts and thus the philosophers are forced to confront the religionists (*ahl al-millah*) for their own safety, maintaining that they are not confronting religion as such, but rather the contention of those religionists that religion indeed contradicts philosophy. Those religionists are then reminded that the propositions on which their religious beliefs rest are no more than representations of genuine philosophical propositions or principles.[9]

8. *Iḥṣā' al-'Ulūm*, p. 131.
9. Ibid., p. 155.

In conclusion, al-Fārābi does not exclude the possibility that certain nations might show some compassion for philosophy, but those nations are overwhelmed by nations who have passed it in silence or prohibit it altogether. The reason for this prohibition is that the nations in question are not fit to be taught the 'unadulterated truth' or theoretical matters in general, but are amenable to instruction simply by recourse to the 'analogies of truth' on practical actions and pursuits. Sometimes, the lawgivers or rulers are willing to go so far as to propagate or defend false religious beliefs or practices for the sole aim of realizing their own well-being or satisfaction, irrespective of the well-being or satisfaction of their subjects.

Presocratics, stoics and peripatetics

A further instance of al-Fārābi's historical erudition is the account he gives, in a short tract entitled *What Ought to Precede the Study of Philosophy* (*Mā Yanbaqhi an Yataqaddam al-Falsafah*), of the various Greek philosophical schools and their founders. Of these schools, he mentions the Pythagorean School and its founder, Pythagoras, the Cyrenaic School founded by Aristippus, the followers of Chryssippus, known as the 'people of the Stoa' because their teaching took place, as he states, in a porch (*ruwāq*) attached to the Temple of Athens. He does not mention, in this context, the name of the actual founder of the Stoic School, Zeno of Citium in Cyprus. This is followed by the Cynic School, founded by Diogenes, whose followers were known as 'dogs' (in Greek, *kuwon*, from which the term *cynic* is derived) because they advocated neglect of civic duties and the love of their kin and brethren, all of which are traits pertaining to dogs.

A further school mentioned by al-Fārābi is that of the Sceptics, followers of Pyrrho (*Furun*), who were called Negators (*Māni'ah*), because they negated the possibility of knowledge and barred people from learning. He then mentions the Hedonists, followers of Epicurus, who held that the basic aim of philosophy is the pleasure attendant upon its study.

The list closes with a reference to the Peripatetics (*Mashsha'iyyun*) or followers of Plato and Aristotle, so called because they used to teach the public while they walked or ambled around (Greek *Peripatein*)[10]. (This account applies to the practice of Aristotle, who lectured on more advanced subjects in the morning at the Lyceum; but does not correctly apply to Plato's.) However, considering al-Fārābi's thesis, to be discussed later, that the Two Sages (*hakīmayn*) were in perfect agreement on all the key issues, this account is not surprising.

Next, al-Fārābi reviews the subject-matter of Aristotle's books in very much the way he does in his *Philosophy of Aristotle* and the *Enumeration of the Sciences*, to be discussed later. He does refer, however, in this tract to the traditional division of Aristotle's works into private or acroamatic, reflected in the Arabic tradition in the designation of the *Physics*, as *al-Samā' al-Ṭabi'ī* (*Physike Akroasis*), and public or exoteric. The only reference to Plato's method of instruction consists in his stipulation that the study of philosophy should be preceded by the mastery of geometry, hence the inscription adorning the entrance to the Academy which read, as given by al-Fārābi, 'None may enter who is not a geometrician.'[11] This stipulation is then contrasted with the teaching of Theophrastus, successor of Aristotle at the head of the Lyceum, that the cultivation of character should precede the study of philosophy. Plato is then quoted as stating that only those pure in heart should approach the pure, a sentiment confirmed by Hippocrates, we are told: if you feed unclean bodies, you only increase their evil propensities. Boethius of Sidon is then mentioned as urging that the study of philosophy should begin with physics, contrary to his student Andronicus, who held that such study should begin with logic.[12]

Plato and his philosophy

Of Plato's thirty-two Dialogues, a fairly large number are known to have been translated into Arabic from Galen's compendia or 'synopses'. Of these Dialogues, the *Timaeus* and the *Laws* are reported to have been

10. *Mā Yanbaqhi an Yuqaddam Qabla Ta'allum al-Falsafah* (Dieterici), p. 50.
11. Ibid., p. 52.
12. Ibid., p. 53. Andronicus of Rhodes (fl. 40 BC) was, as mentioned, the editor of Aristotle's writings and the eleventh head of the Lyceum. Boethius was his pupil. Cf. W. Windelband, *History of Ancient Philosophy*, pp. 302f.

translated by Yaḥia Ibn al-Bitriq and subsequently by Hunayn Ibn Ishāq and Yaḥia Ibn 'Adi. The *Crito*, the *Parmenides*, the *Republic*, the *Phaedo*, the *Cratylus*, the *Euthydemus* and the *Sophist* were translated by Ḥunayn Ibn Ishāq and his disciple 'Isā Ibn Yaḥia in conjunction.[13] Most of these translations have not survived, except for the *Laws*, the *Timaeus*, and fragments from the *Phaedo*, the *Apology* and the *Crito*.

In his treatise the *Philosophy of Plato, Its Parts and the Order of Its Parts*, al-Fārābi appears to be fully conversant with these translations in addition to some other Greek source, which may have embodied a summary of the subject-matter of all the *Dialogues* in an Arabic translation. He begins his exposition of Plato's philosophy by an account of his statement in the *Alcibiades* that human perfection does not consist in a sound body, good looks, political office, prosperity, a noble birth or a large company of friends and kin. That perfection, with which human happiness is bound up, consists instead in acquiring genuine knowledge (*'ilm*) and leading a virtuous way of life (*sīrah*).[14]

As for genuine knowledge, it lies, as Plato states in the *Theaetetus*, we are told by al-Fārābi, in the knowledge of the essences of existing things; whereas the virtuous way of life consists in performing those actions conducive to happiness, as Plato states in the *Philebus*. (Elsewhere,[15] al-Fārābi identifies man's perfection with the knowledge of God, His unity, wisdom and justice, adding that the true philosopher is one who 'seeks likeness unto God (*homoiosis Theō*) as far as is humanly possible', as Plato actually states in *Theaetetus*, 176 *b*. In further investigating the nature of genuine knowledge, we are then told by al-Fārābi, Plato rebuts the claim of Protagoras the Sophist, in the Dialogue called by his name, that genuine knowledge is not possible, but only opinion (*doxa*, *ẓann*). He, then, inquires in the *Meno* whether genuine knowledge is acquired by instruction or is simply a matter of chance, so that what is unknown will remain forever unknown or unknowable, as Meno contends in that *Dialogue*.[16]

13. See M. Fakhry, *A History of Islamic Philosophy*, p. 13.
14. *Falsafah Aflātun*, p. 3.
15. *Mā Yanbaqhi an Yataqaddam al-Falsafah* (Dieterici), p. 53.
16. Ibid., p. 6. Cf. *Meno*, 80, where the focus of the discussion is actually whether virtue is teachable or not.

Having refuted that view, we are told, Plato then proceeds to identify the kind of inquiry (*faḥs*) that could lead to genuine knowledge. In reviewing the various opinions entertained by various nations, he begins with the religious (*diyāniyah*) inquiry, and asks whether that inquiry, or the 'syllogistic religious art' (by which al-Fārābi probably meant theology ['*ilm al-kalām*], is adequate or not. He concludes in the *Euthyphro*, we are told, that inquiry and that art are not able to yield genuine knowledge or lead to a virtuous way of life.[17]

Plato then turns in the *Cratylus* to the claim of the linguists that genuine knowledge can be attained by mastering words and their connotations as understood by the people who speak a given language; so that one who masters those connotations will have acquired the knowledge of the essences of things. This linguistics view is rejected by Plato, too. Plato then inquires, according to al-Fārābi, whether poetry, the art of versification or the faculty of reciting poetry, as well as understanding the meaning of poetic odes and the maxims they embody, can yield genuine knowledge or contribute to the pursuit of a virtuous mode of life. He concludes in the *Ion*, we are told, that the common poetic method is far from being able to lead to the attainment of these two goals, the theoretical and the practical, but rather the contrary.[18]

It is well-known how vehement was Plato in his condemnation of poetry as a debased imitation of reality twice removed. For the poets, by whom he meant the mythological poets, such as Homer and Hesiod, have ascribed shameful actions to the gods or represented them as able, like magicians, to appear in various forms, human or otherwise. For, as Plato puts it in the *Republic*, 'the divine nature must be perfect in every way and would therefore be the last thing to suffer transformation'.[19] Al-Fārābi, however, does not dwell here or elsewhere, as far as we know, on this critical assessment of the nature of poetry by Plato. Next, Plato investigates the rhetorical and sophistical methods in the *Gorgias*, the *Sophist* and the *Euthydemus*, respectively, and shows, according to al-Fārābi, that neither one of these methods is capable of attaining the two goals of

17. Ibid., p. 6.
18. Ibid., p. 7.
19. *Republic*, II, 380 d *et passim*.

knowledge and virtue. He goes so far in his critique of the Sophists, we are told, as to describe their method of instruction as mere sport (*la'ib*) which does not lead to profitable knowledge, whether theoretical or practical.[20]

As for dialectic (*jadal*), Plato shows in the *Parmenides*, according to al-Fārābi, that this art is very useful in serving a prefatory or propaedeutic function. Indeed, he believes, that one cannot acquire genuine knowledge without prior training in dialectic.

Having completed the examination of the common theoretical means of attaining knowledge and virtue, Plato then turned to the practical arts, but found in *Alcibiades* II (Minor), according to al-Fārābi, that what the public regards as virtuous or profitable action is not really so. In the *Hipparchus*, he shows that the only profitable and useful arts consist in that knowledge and that virtuous way of life with which human perfection is bound up; but none of the common practical arts is capable of leading to that 'true perfection'.[21]

Some have argued, al-Fārābi goes on, that human perfection can be attained by adopting that way of life affected by the Hypocrites and the Sophists, who reveal what they conceal meticulously. Plato has condemned these ways, we are told, in two books called after two famous Sophists, who excelled in the art of hypocricy and disputation, called *Hippias* I (Major) and *Hippias* II (Minor). Plato then inquires, we are next told, whether the goal of human perfection can be attained by pursuing the life of pleasure, as the Hedonists claim, and concludes that that goal is not attainable by means of the ways of life affected by the Hedonists, in his book *On Pleasure*, attributed to Socrates.[22]

In the second part of the *Philosophy of Plato*, al-Fārābi dwells on Plato's specific determination of the two genuine theoretical and practical arts, which alone can lead to the desired goal of genuine knowledge and a virtuous life conducive to happiness. That goal, according to Plato in the *Theages*, can only be attained by means of the theoretical art, which he identifies with philosophy. As for the practical art that leads to the desired goal of a virtuous life and directs one's actions towards happiness, Plato

20. Ibid., p. 9.
21. Ibid., p. 11.
22. This is probably a reference to the *Philebus*.

has shown it, according to al-Fārābi, to be politics or the 'royal art'. He has also shown that the philosopher and the king are one and the same, since they are both 'perfected by the same skill or faculty and each one of them possesses the same skill which imparts the desired genuine knowledge and the desired virtuous way of life conducive to true happiness'.[23]

This leads Plato, we are then told by al-Fārābi, to investigate the nature of temperance in the *Charmides*, that of courage in the *Laches*, followed by love and friendship in the *Phaedrus*. Love, he argues, sometimes reaches the pitch of erotic passion (*'ishq*), which can lead to madness, whether human or divine. The latter is a disposition of the 'divine soul', reports al-Fārābi, to yearn after divine things; whereas the former is a disposition of the human soul to seek the satisfaction of 'beastly' passion and renounce divine things. This form of passion is clearly unworthy of the philosopher-king.[24] He also discusses in that *Dialogue* the means of achieving the philosophical goal and the degree to which rhetoric and dialectic, whether verbal or written, can contribute towards that goal.

In the *Crito*, we are then told that it is characteristic of philosophers that thay will not acquiesce in the conventions of their compatriots or their ways, but will constantly seek truth in theoretical matters, and virtue in practical matters. Thus, they will be prepared to brave all dangers in the pursuit of these two goals, and, should they despair of leading the life of knowledge and virtue in the manner of beasts, they will prefer death to life. That is why, Plato argues in the *Apology of Socrates* and the *Phaedo*, that the unexamined life is not worth living and that one who cannot lead a life worthy of humankind will prefer death to life, as Socrates does in those two Dialogues.

For this reason, Plato was led to maintain, according to al-Fārābi, that a city other than existing cities and a nation other than existing nations are needed and this led him to investigate the nature of that city whose essential characteristic is justice. When he proceeded to investigate the nature of justice, he found that common justice, practiced in the cities of his day, was no better than sheer evil. To rid the world of evils rampant in

23. Ibid., p. 13.
24. Ibid., p. 15. Cf. *Phaedrus*, 245f.

cities around him, al-Fārābi says, he felt he had to construct another (ideal) city in which true justice and the true goods that are essential for the happiness of its inhabitants and the royal art of philosophy reign supreme. In such a city, the philosophers will form the noblest class, followed by the lower classes of guardians and artisans discussed in the *Republic*, but which al-Fārābi does not mention in this context.

As for the methods of instructing the inhabitants of the virtuous city and the laws that should govern them, Plato dealt with these questions, according to al-Fārābi, in the *Laws*, the *Critias* and the *Timaeus*. In speaking of the methods of instruction, al-Fārābi compares the method used by Socrates to that used by Thrasymachus, the Sophist, mentioned in the first book of the *Republic*. Although in that book, Plato is vehement in his critique of the sophistical method and especially Thrasymachus's definition of justice as the right of the stronger party, al-Fārābi is rather conciliatory in contrasting the two views. The method of Thrasymachus, he says, is more effective in instructing the youth and the public in general; whereas the Socratic method is more suitable for the scientific investigation of justice and the remaining virtues, but not for instructing the youth and the public at large. For al-Fārābi, however, the philosopher, the king and the lawgiver must be capable of practicing both methods, that of Socrates in dealing with the élite (*khāṣṣah*) and that of Thrasymachus in dealing with the youth and the public at large.[25]

Al-Fārābi concludes the *Philosophy of Plato* with a brief reference to Plato's *Letters*, of which seven have survived. In these letters, according to al-Fārābi, Plato refers to the cities and the nations that existed in his day and reiterates his grand thesis that the perfect human, the questioning human and the virtuous human are always in grave danger and that their only salvation consists in reforming those cities and prevailing on their inhabitants to change their ways. He has used as his model in calling for such reform, we are told by al-Fārābi, the people of Athens, his own compatriots, and their commendable ways of life (*siyār*).[26]

This rather sketchy outline is impressive for its scope. In it, al-Fārābi highlights Plato's conception of the theoretical and practical goals of life,

25. Ibid., p. 22.
26. Ibid., p. 23.

the organic relation of philosophy and politics, the 'royal art', and his attitude to the Sophists, the poets and the linguists. It does not do justice to his theory of Ideas, as given in the *Republic* and the *Timaeus*, his view of knowledge as recollection, as given in the *Phaedrus*, or of immortality as developed in the *Phaedo*. Equally surprising is al-Fārābi's passing in silence Plato's cosmological views, embodied in the *Timaeus*, which was translated into Arabic by Ḥunayn Ibn Ishāq and his associates and has survived in Galen's compendium;[27] especially since this Dialogue dwells at length on the creation of the universe in time by the Demiurgus (*al-Sāni'*), a favorite theme of the Mutakallimun. What is puzzling is al-Fārābi's apparent acquaintance with all the *Dialogues* and the *Letters*, especially since only a small part of the *Dialogues*, as we have seen, and none of the *Letters* had been translated into Arabic. The only possible explanation is that he had access to some summary in Arabic, which listed the works of Plato and discussed them briefly and is now no longer extant; or that he came into contact with some Syriac scholar fluent in Greek who initiated him into the secrets of Plato's philosophy.

Be this as it may, we have a much more positive instance of al-Fārābi's Platonic scholarship in his compendium or summary of the *Laws* (*Talkhīs Nawāmīs Aflāṭun*), which is extant. He opens this summary by stating in the preface that Plato, the Sage (*Hakīm*), as he puts it, did not wish to disclose the knowledge of the various sciences to everybody, and thus adopted the method of symbolism or mystification, so that the knowledge of these sciences is not made accessible to those who are unworthy of it; and is thereby demeaned. Later on, when that method became widely known, Plato abandoned it and proceeded to express himself in clear terms. This double method has created confusion in the minds of the learned, as his style in the *Laws* shows. For this reason, al-Fārābi says, he decided to extract the hidden meanings of that book, so as to assist its reader and spare him the time and the trouble of studying or meditating on it.[28]

With this, he proceeds to summarize nine of the books of the *Laws* one by one, commenting at the end of Book IX that those were the parts

27. Cf. edition and Latin translation of P. Kraus and R. Walzer, *Galeni Compendium Timaei Platonis* (London: Warburg Institute, 1951).
28. *Talkhīs Nawāmīs Aflāṭun*, p. 3.

accessible to him, the rest being unknown to him. He indicates that the total number of the books of the *Laws* is in dispute, some putting it at ten, others at fourteen.[29] The traditional number of the books of the *Laws* is actually twelve.

Like Plato, al-Fārābi opens Book I by referring to the question of the Athenian about the identity of the author of the laws, to which the answer given by Clinias is that, for the Athenians, this author is Zeus (*Zāwush*), identified by al-Fārābi with the father of humankind. He then refers to the great advantages gained by instituting the laws, as a means of securing peace and friendship among the citizens of the state, instead of struggle or warfare.[30] He then refers to Plato's thesis that the chief goal of the lawgiver is the cultivation of the four virtues – wisdom, courage, temperance and justice – and how these virtues are divisible into two parts, human and divine. The former include good looks, bodily strength, wealth and knowledge, which, when subordinated to the laws of the land, become divine.[31]

In Book II, we are told by al-Fārābi, Plato discusses the right means of instilling virtue in the souls of the citizens, by appealing to the natural proclivity of humankind to seek pleasure and avoid pain, especially where the young are concerned. The lawgiver should thus regulate pleasurable pursuits, such as music and dancing, encourage whatever actions conduce to virtue and discourage whatever is conducive to vice.[32]

In Book III, we are told, Plato speaks of the founding of the city-state (*polis*), which should rest on a solid moral foundation and in which wisdom should reign. Thus the lawgiver should accord reason and education the greatest attention. To be well-governed, such a city-state must be ruled by the oldest, most virtuous and most experienced class of citizens. This theme is pursued in Book IV, where Plato reaffirms the need for a 'divine ruler', intent on inculcating virtuous and noble traits in the souls of his subjects. Such a ruler will not resort to repressive measures, except in dealing with evil or unruly elements in the state.

29. Ibid., p. 43.
30. Ibid., p. 6. Cf. *Laws*, I, 628 *d*.
31. Ibid., p. 8. Cf. *Laws*, I, 631 *c*.
32. Ibid., p. 14. Cf. *Laws*, II, 653.

In Book V, Plato, we are told, speaks of the soul as the most divine element in the human being, the element that should therefore be favored next to God. It is incumbent on the lawgiver to lay down the laws of caring for the soul and the body and the ways in which the cardinal virtues of justice, temperance and courage are instilled in the soul through a process of habituation.

As for the state itself, Plato shows in the *Laws*, according to al-Fārābi, that its excellence consists in moderation, in such a way that none of its needs in territory, foodstuffs or temples, as determined by the lawgiver, should be in excess or defect. It is imperative, he adds, that such a lawgiver should be as concerned about the welfare of the rich as well as that of the poor.

In Book VI, we are told, Plato argues that the virtuous city should be well-ordered and great care should be exercised in the choice of its rulers, as well as the ministers or counselors serving them, whether in time of war or peace. The universal rule in dealing with the public is equality, by which should not be understood the equality of slaves and freemen, but rather the duty of treating equals equally and unequals unequally.[33]

In Book VII, we are then told, Plato deals with the records bequeathed by the lawgiver, as a testimony that should not be tampered with; while in Book VIII, he deals with legislation governing the festivals, dedicated to glorifying the gods, followed by discussion of sacrifices and the rules governing them. The virtuous inhabitants of the city are those who accustom themselves to comply with the laws of the city and their subsidiary provisions, such as visiting the temples and keeping the company of the virtuous. He then refers to the way in which the wicked, who do not honor the houses of worship, the elderly or the rulers, should be punished. He then shows that the virtuous have no need for laws or regulations which are intended for those of base character.

As for the punishments meted out to the wicked in both this world and the world-to-come, especially to those who have not been raised to respect the laws, or those who engage in sacrilegious activities, they may appear on the surface to be unjust, but are for Plato fully justified.[34]

33. Ibid., p. 32; *Laws*, VI, 757 *b*.
34. Ibid., p. 42. Cf. *Laws* IX, 880f.

The philosophy of Aristotle

In *The Philosophy of Aristotle, Its Parts and the Order of Its Parts*, al-Fārābi attempts to give a comprehensive account of the divisions of Aristotle's philosophy and the subject-matter of his various writings, more or less in the same way as he does in the *Philosophy of Plato*, already discussed. He begins by laying down as a premise that for Aristotle the perfection of humankind cannot be attained by the knowledge of what is natural or that which is voluntary in isolation, but by the two in conjunction. Now, insofar as nature precedes will, it is incumbent on us to begin by investigating things that exist by nature and then things that exist by will or choice, so as to gain knowledge of both natural and voluntary things or activities. It was for this reason that Aristotle believed, according to al-Fārābi, that the inquiry should start with the determination of the nature and divisions of certain knowledge (*yaqīn*) and how it differs from opinion (*ẓann*), as well as the other subordinate degrees of assent, such as imagination and persuasion. He then turns to the discussion of the methods of instruction appropriate to each class of people and the various modes of address (*mukhāṭabah*) and sophistical discourse (*muqhalāṭah*). This is what Aristotle undertook, we are told, in the art of logic, which precedes the two sciences of the natural and the voluntary; i.e. the theoretical and practical sciences.[35]

The logical treatises begin, al-Fārābi goes on, with the *Categories* (*Qātiguriās*), which deal with simple terms, followed by *On Interpretation* (*Bārmānias, Peri Hermeneias*), which deals with propositions, then the *First Analytics (Kitāb al-Qiyās* or *Anālūtiqa al-Ūlā*), which deals with syllogisms (sing. *qiyās*), and then the *Second Analytics* (*Kitāb al-Burhān* or *Apodeictica*), which deals with certain knowledge, which is alone worthy of the name of wisdom (*ḥikmah*) or genuine science (*'ilm*).

The analytical or demonstrative part of logic is followed, according to al-Fārābi, by the two 'gymnastic' arts (*riyāḍiyat*), consisting of dialectic (*jadal*) and sophistical discourse (*muqhātabah*). The sophistical methods used to silence the adversary are then given as six: reprimand (*tabkīt*), confounding (*tahyīr*), stunning (*baht*), incapacity (*'ayy*), babbling (*hadhr*) and silencing (*iskāt*).[36]

35. *Falsafat Aristutālīs*, pp. 70f.
36. Ibid., p. 81. Cf. *Sophistical Refutations*, 181 *b* 10f.

In *Rhetorica* and *Poetica*, Aristotle discusses, according to al-Fārābi, the methods used by those who are unable to master the scientific methods of logic or attain certainty, owing to some natural impediment or preoccupation with false pursuits.

In his own treatise on rhetoric, al-Fārābi develops further this theme, according to which persuasion (*iqnā'*) in all the ten categories is attempted in the same way as dialectic, which is historically posterior to rhetoric, as we have seen in his account of the genesis of philosophy. For speakers originally used rhetorical methods of discourse, followed by dialectical and sophistical methods, and this state of affairs continued until the time of Plato, who distinguished the dialectical from the sophistical, rhetorical and poetical methods. However, he stopped short of laying down the universal rules of demonstration, as Aristotle did in his *Analytica Posteriora* (*Kitāb al-Burhān*). From that time on, philosophers abandoned the old methods, but continued to use dialectic for purposes of exercise, sophistry for purposes of examination or admonition and rhetoric in matters common to all the arts and the instruction of the public in non-specific matters or political interactions.[37]

As for poetical discourse, al-Fārābi explains in his *Paraphrase of Poetica* along essentially Aristotelian lines that the aim of poetry is simulation (*muhākāt, mimesis*) by recourse to actions or words, leading the observer to imagine the matter at hand. That is why, he explains, imagination is analogous to science in demonstration, opinion in dialectic and persuasion in rhetoric, all of which form part of the syllogistic arts, according to al-Fārābi.[38] This is what justifies, in his opinion, the inclusion of poetics and rhetoric in the logical corpus, as was the case in the Syriac and Arabic traditions, as will be shown in Chapter 4.

Logic is, then, an art that lays down the rules of reasoning, whether demonstrative, dialectical or sophistical, and serves as a propaedeutic to the study of the substantive sciences of physics, metaphysics, politics and ethics. It is for this reason that al-Fārābi proceeds next in his *Philosophy of Aristotle* to discuss the 'science of physics'. He observes rightly that Aristotle has given in his *Physics* certain universal principles, expressed in

37. *Kitāb al-Khatābah*, in *Deux Ouvrages Inédits sur la Rhétorique*, pp. 55f.
38. *Jawāmi' al-Shi'r*, p. 172.

the form of universal propositions, premises and laws common to all natural entities.[39] Of these principles or premises, he mentions the universal laws of being, peculiar to corporeal substances, what they are and why. To each of these substances correspond a potential principle which he called matter and an actual principle which he called form. For the potential principle to become actualized, we are told by al-Fārābi, Aristotle stipulated that it requires an active principle, or cause. He then proceeded to show that, with respect to every movable or changeable entity, four essential principles or causes are needed: the material, efficient, formal and final causes.

Next, Aristotle turned to the definition of nature, as conceived by the ancient (Ionian) naturalists (actually discussed in Aristotle's first book of the *Physics* and in *Generation and Corruption*). This led him to the discussion of extension as an essential property of physical objects and the view that it is impossible for these objects to extend *ad infinitum* in magnitude or bulk.

Next, Aristotle investigated, according to al-Fārābi, the nature of motion, which is an attribute of all physical objects and involves physical transition at a distance and in time. This led him to investigate the nature of place and of time. He concluded that place is inseparable from body, but rejected the view of those who (like Democritus and Leucippus) posited the void as a pre-condition of motion. As for time, he inquired whether natural objects in motion must exist in time; or whether time is an attribute of objects which is not essential for their existence. Here, al-Fārābi omits to mention the famous definition of time as the 'number of motion' with respect to before and after.[40]

The investigation of motion led Aristotle, according to al-Fārābi, to posit a series of movers that are in contact with each other and terminate in a 'finite body which moves all physical objects' and is the mover of the spheres.[41] This mover, identified by Aristotle with the first heaven or outermost sphere,[42] imparts to the heavenly spheres their motions, which

39. Ibid., p. 92.
40. *Physics*, II, 219 *b* 11.
41. *Falsafat Arisṭuṭālis*, p. 96.
42. *Metaphysics*, XII, 1072 *a* 20.

in turn cause the motions of physical bodies in the lower world. However, this first mover derives its motion ultimately from an entity that is neither a body nor inheres in a body, but is entirely immaterial and incorporeal. Its investigation, says al-Fārābi, pertains to a science other than physics;[43] namely, metaphysics. Al-Fārābi is clearly referring here to the Unmoved Mover, who is stated in *Metaphysics*, XII, 1072 b f. to be the ultimate principle of motion, in substance and actuality; in fact is the actuality of thought thinking itself, or, as al-Fārābi has expressed it in the *Virtuous City*, *'aql, āqil and ma'qūl.*

The science of physics led Aristotle, according to al-Fārābi, to posit four primary and simple elements, from which all material bodies in the lower world are made up and which depend on a fifth element (i.e. ether), which is the cause of the existence of the four. This element constitutes the substance of the heavenly bodies that act on physical objects here-below and cause their generation and corruption, as he has shown, we are told, in *De Coelo et Mundo* (*al-Samā' wa'l-'Ālam*).[44]

The varying processes of generation and corruption are then discussed in the *Generation and Corruption*, the *Meterologica* (*al-Āthār al-'Ulawiyah*), the *Book of Minerals*, his spurious book *On Plants*, and the zoological corpus, known to the Arabs in nineteen books, which al-Fārābi alludes to, but does not mention by name.

Having concluded the discussion of the various processes of generation and corruption culminating in the lower organic forms of life, i.e. plants and animals, Aristotle proceeds, we are told, to discuss the soul, which actually formed part of the science of physics for Aristotle.

In his discussion of the soul, we are then told, Aristotle was led to conclude that the soul, considered in relation to living organisms, is a principle, *qua* agent, *qua* form and *qua* end. However, al-Fārābi stops short here of giving Aristotle's famous definition of the soul, as the first perfection (*istikmāl*, *entelecheia*) of a natural, organic body capable of life,[45] which he gives nonetheless in one of his shorter treatises.[46] This is

43. *Falsafat Arisṭuṭālīs*, p. 97.
44. Ibid., p. 99.
45. *De anima*, II, 412 *b* 30.
46. *Fī Jawāb Masā'il* (Dieterici), p. 79. Cf. *Kitāb al-Burhān*, p. 48.

followed by a discussion of those actions or affections of the soul dealt with in the *Parva Naturalia*, known to the Arabs as *Sense and Sensibles* (*Kitāb al-Ḥiss wa'l-Mahsūs*), of which a large part was known to the Arabs. Those actions and affections include health and sickness, youth and old age, life and death, sleep and divination by dreams, memory and recollection. In discussing divination by dreams, we are told by al-Fārābi, Aristotle observed that the natural powers of the soul are not sufficient to explain those prognostications and forebodings which warn of future events. Therefore, he dealt with this subject elsewhere.[47]

Here, al-Fārābi reverses the order of discussing the faculties of the soul and proceeds to summarize Aristotle's theory of the intellect (*'aql*), to which he has devoted a substantial treatise, which will be discussed later. In the context of the *Philosophy of Aristotle*, he is content to state that the intellect was regarded by Aristotle as the essential differentia of humankind, as distinct from other animals endowed with lower sensitive faculties, such as sense-perception and imagination. Aristotle then reduces the activities of the intellect to two kinds, theoretical and practical. The latter, Aristotle held, we are told, are subservient to the former, to the extent that the theoretical intellect is superior to the practical. When he proceeds to discuss how the intellect is actualized, he observes that the potential intellect is in possession of certain first principles or intelligibles, which exist in it by nature, although it has received them from a higher intellect, which is always in act. This is the Active Intellect (*al-'Aql al-Fa'āl*), upon which the whole process of human cognition depends. It is 'the immaterial faculty, the immaterial end, the immaterial agent of mankind, to which mankind is conjoined in a certain sense'.[48] It is, indeed, the perfection towards which humankind should aspire.

Conjunction (*ittisāl*) with or, as he sometimes puts it, proximity (*muqāraba*, *qurb*) to this intellect, as we shall see in the discussion of al-Fārābi's theory of knowledge, is the warrant of the actualization of humankind's cognitive powers. It has in addition a cosmic function, which

47. Al-Fārābi does not mention where; but in *Divination by Dreams* Aristotle deals with what he calls 'prophetic dreams', which he describes as mere coincidences. Cf. *Divination by Dreams*, 463 *b*.
48. Ibid., p. 128.

is nowhere stated explicitly by Aristotle, but was really part of the Neoplatonic tradition, which al-Fārābi, as we have seen, was the first to introduce into the Muslim world. Thus, Aristotle goes on to ask, according to al-Fārābi, whether the Active Intellect is also the cause of the existence of nature, of natural or inanimate entities, of the soul and animate entities in general. What led Aristotle to raise this question, we are told, was his earlier assertion that the heavenly bodies are the principles that move the simple elements and compounds in the lower world, but not without the assistance (*murāfadah*) of the Active Intellect. For he held that the heavenly bodies are incapable of generating by themselves the world of nature, of soul or reason,[49] but only the motions in which they are involved. However, the essence of those heavenly bodies, and whether they are certain natures, souls or reasons, lies outside the scope of the science of physics. For this science terminates, al-Fārābi writes, with the Active Intellect and the mover of the heavenly bodies.[50] He does not specify here who that mover is, but in his *Treatise on the Intellect*, which will be discussed later, al-Fārābi states that because the action of the Active Intellect is neither continuous nor constant, and is dependent to some extent on the material substrata on which it acts, it is clearly distinguishable from the First Principle (or God), upon whom it ultimately depends.[51] For Aristotle, on the other hand, the action of the First Principle is mediated by that of the first moved mover (*primus mobile*), which he identifies with the first heaven or the outermost sphere, and which derives its motion ultimately from the First Principle, who is unmoved, hence his designation as the Unmoved Mover.[52]

Without dwelling on the nature of that science which lies beyond physics, al-Fārābi concludes his exposition with a brief reference to the way in which the practical intellect, concerned with volition and choice, subserves the theoretical, wherein human perfection consists. However, instead of turning to the ethics of Aristotle, on which he is known to have written a commentary which is no longer extant, he reiterates his statement that the physical inquiry cannot proceed beyond the Active

49. Ibid., p. 129.
50. Ibid., p. 130.
51. *Risālah fi'l-'Aql*, pp. 33f.
52. See Aristotle, *Physics*, *VIII*, 267 *a* 20f. and *Metaphysics*, *XII*, 1072 *a* 20f.

Intellect and the heavenly bodies. More specifically, this inquiry leads to the conclusion that all humankind's natural faculties, including the practical, rational faculties, exist for the sake of humankind's theoretical perfection. However, al-Fārābi observes, human rational nature is not complete without those actions which arise from will and choice, associated with practical reason; hence, the ethical inquiry into what is good and useful. However, neither the 'physical nor the human sciences' are adequate for the purpose of attaining humankind's theoretical perfection; hence the need to engage in the discussion of those entities which lie above natural entities in rank. Accordingly, Aristotle engaged in the discussion of those higher entities in a science he called 'what lies after physics' (*mā ba'd al-ṭabī'iyāh; meta ta physica*).[53]

With this terse statement, the discussion is closed. Significantly, however, al-Fārābi has discussed the divisions and subject-matter of metaphysics or the 'divine science', as he calls it, in a more systematic treatise entitled the *Enumeration of the Sciences* (*Iḥṣā' al-Ulūm*), which forms the subject-matter of the next chapter, and in the *Intentions of Aristotle in the Metaphysics* as well.

The harmony of Plato and Aristotle

Al-Fārābi opens his treatise on the *Reconciliation of the Opinions of the Two Sages* (*al-Jam 'bayna Ra'yay al-Hakīmayn*) by explaining that his reason for undertaking this task is the fact that he had observed 'that most of our contemporaries' are at loggerheads on the questions of the eternity or temporality (*hudūth*) of the universe and have gone so far as to allege that the 'foremost sages' (i.e. Plato and Aristotle) are in disagreement on such questions as the existence of the Creator, the nature of the soul and the intellect, the reward and punishment of right and wrong actions, as well as numerous ethical, political and logical questions.

He begins by positing as a first premise that the definition of philosophy or its essence is that it is the knowledge of existing entities,

53. Ibid., p. 132. This expression was not Aristotle's, who calls this higher science 'first philosophy', *theologia*, or ontology. The expression was coined by his editor, Andronicus of Rhodes, to refer to the treatise that comes *after* the physics.

insofar as they exist. This is followed by the second premise that it is the Two Sages who have laid down its foundations and actually perfected it. If this is the case, then, their alleged disagreement can only be due to one of three things: 1) either the above definition is false, or 2) the widespread consensus of the majority of scholars regarding the philosophical contribution of the Two Sages is tenuous or doubtful, or 3) the alleged disagreement between them is due to ignorance or poor judgment (*taqsīr*) on the part of its advocates.

Now, the first alternative is clearly unwarranted, as the investigation of the various parts of philosophy, whether in logic, physics, metaphysics or politics, clearly shows. The second alternative is equally unwarranted, for the consensus (*ijtimā'*)[54] of learned scholars is known with certainty to be conclusive evidence for the truthfulness of their positions. This leaves the third alternative; namely, that those who allege that there is any disagreement on fundamentals (*usūl*) between the Two Sages suffer actually from ignorance or poor judgment, as al-Fārābi then proceeds to show.

In support of this thesis, he begins by conceding that there were indeed certain differences of temper or demeanor between the Two Sages, such as Plato's otherworldliness and contempt for earthly possessions, as contrasted with Aristotle's worldliness, as illustrated by his marriage, his service to Alexander, the king, and his amassing of fortune. All this, however, does not justify the claim that they were at odds regarding their respective conceptions of moral probity and political organization. It simply shows that there were some differences between their two modes of life, stemming from 'a certain deficiency in philosophical powers of one and an excess of (these powers) in the other',[55] al-Fārābi states cryptically.

Equally noteworthy are the different methods of writing and instruction adopted by the Two Sages; Plato is known to have favored the use of allegory and symbolism to shield his views from those who are unworthy of them, while Aristotle favored clarity and systematism in expounding his views. However, it should be admitted that those alleged differences are relative, since Aristotle himself sometimes resorts to allegory and symbolism in some of his metaphysical and ethical writings.

54. *Ijtimā'* derives from the same root as *ijmā'*, but does not have the same legalistic force.
55. *Al-Jam' Bayna Ra'yay al-Hakīmayn* (Dieterici), p. 5.

Most pertinent, perhaps, is al-Fārābi's reference to the divergent views of Plato and Aristotle regarding substance (*jawhar*), which Plato is thought to have identified with the intelligible and supersensible universal (Idea), while Aristotle identified it with the individual or particular. This alleged divergence, according to al-Fārābi, owes to the context in which the issue was discussed by the two; Aristotle dealt with it in his logical and physical treatises, whereas Plato dealt with it in his metaphysical writings, 'where one is concerned with simple and durable entities which do not change and do not cease to exist'.[56]

Having dealt with these methodological differences between the Two Sages, al-Fārābi turns next to the substantive differences between them on the questions of vision, moral traits, theory of knowledge, the soul and its destiny, the eternity of the world and the status of universals or Ideas.

The most important of these questions from a historical point of view was that of the eternity of the world, which was at the center of violent theological and philosophical controversies in both the East and West, as illustrated by the classic controversy between al-Ghazāli and Averroes, on the one hand, and St. Thomas Aquinas and the Latin Averroists in Paris, on the other.

Aristotle is alleged, al-Fārābi writes, to hold that the world is eternal (*qadīm*) and Plato to have held that it is created in time (*muḥdath*). What has led to this 'repugnant and awful opinion', says al-Fārābi, is the fact that Aristotle states in *Topica* 'that there are certain propositions of which each side may be supported by a syllogism based on generally accepted premises; for example, this world is eternal or not'.[57] He also states in *De Coelo et Mundo* (as the *Heavens* was called in the Arabic sources) that the 'whole has no temporal beginning', from which it was wrongly inferred that he believed the world to be eternal. It is not realized, however, argues al-Fārābi, that Aristotle's purpose, in the case of the first statement given in *Topica*, is not to determine the temporal status of the universe, but rather to give a (formal) instance of a syllogism made up of generally accepted premises. In the case of his statement in the *Heavens*, he did not

56. Ibid., p. 8. Of Plato's writings, al-Fārābi mentions here the *Timaeus* and the *Statesman*; of Aristotle's, the *Categories* and the *Physics*.
57. Ibid., p. 23. Cf. *Topica*, 104 *b* 15.

intend to prove that the world is eternal, but rather the contrary, since he has shown in that book and in other physical and metaphysical writings that time is the measure of the motion of the sphere from which it is generated. Now what is generated from something is not contained in that thing. Therefore, by his statement that the world has no temporal beginning should be understood that it was not generated bit by bit, every part of which succeeding the other, as a house or an animal is generated, but rather at once, by an act of divine creation (*ibdā'*), without any reference to time. It was from the motion of the world that time was then generated.[58]

In confirmation of this interpretation of Aristotle's view of the status of the universe, al-Fārābi then refers the reader to the *Book of Divinity* (*Kitāb al-Rubūbiyah*) or the spurious *Theologia Aristotelis*. In that book, which is known today to be a paraphrase of Plotinus's last three *Enneads*, matter, according to al-Fārābi, is said to have been created by God out of nothing by an act of divine fiat. He then proceeds to support this thesis by reference to other Neoplatonic writings, such as a well-known treatise of Ammonius (Saccas), Plotinus's own teacher, 'which is too known to refer to in this context'.[59] He even goes so far as to assert that none of the religious creeds or laws, whether Magian, Jewish or other, has been able to explain the coming-to-be or cessation of the world in a satisfactory way; so that 'were it not for God's mercy in rescuing the minds of thoughtful people from error, thanks to those Two Sages and their followers, who have interpreted creation clearly and convincingly, as an act of bringing something out of nothing',[60] al-Fārābi writes, humankind would have remained forever in a state of confusion and uncertainty.

In this subtle, but questionable interpretation of Aristotle's view of the generation of the world in time and *ex nihilo*, it is probable that al-Fārābi was continuing a Neoplatonic tradition initiated by Porphyry of Tyre (d. 304), who is known to have written a treatise entitled *That the Views of Plato and Aristotle Are the Same*,[61] which probably dealt with the question of

58. Ibid., p. 23.
59. Ibid., p. 25.
60. Ibid., p. 26.
61. Cf. Suidas, *Lexicon, II*, 2, 373 and Ueberweg, *History of Philosophy*, English trans., New York, 1894, p. 251.

eternity and non-eternity in the same conciliatory spirit as al-Fārābi's. It is unquestioned, however, that Plato and Aristotle were completely at loggerheads on the question of the eternity or non-eternity of the world. In the *Metaphysics*, Aristotle is axiomatic that substances, by which he meant the totality of existing entities, 'are the first of existing things; and if they are all destructible, all things would be destructible'.[62] It is impossible, he adds, that motion and time, which he describes as the number of motion, should be destructible, or else there would be a time when time was not or a time when time will not be, which he believed to be absurd.

Plato, by contrast, posited in his great cosmological dialogue, the *Timaeus*, a Creator, whom he called the *Demiurgus* (or *Artisan*), who created the world out of a formless matter, which he calls the 'receptacle' or the 'nurse of all generation'.[63] For him, the Ideas that form the archetypes of this creation were eternal and immutable, but the world itself was subject to constant flux. Time itself, which Plato calls the moving image of eternity, came into being together with the heavens; for, as he puts it, 'time, then and the heavens came into being at the same instant in order that, having been created together, they might be dissolved together';[64] a prospect that Plato, in fact, excluded, holding that once created in time, the universe was actually everlasting. In short, for him, the world has a beginning, but no end.

It is to be noted, as historically significant, that the same interpretation was attempted two centuries later by the great Jewish Aristotelian, Moses Maimonides (d. 1204), in his *Guide of the Perplexed* (*Dalālat al-Hā'irīn*), written originally in Arabic. Here, Maimonides is out to exonerate Aristotle from the charge of adhering to the thesis of eternity and quotes the same passages from *Topica* and *De Coelo* cited by al-Fārābi. For Maimonides, Aristotle has no *demonstrative* proof that the world is eternal and cannot for that reason be charged with adhering to that thesis. It is puzzling, however, that Maimonides, who had a lot of regard for al-Fārābi, goes on to attribute to him the contrary thesis that Aristotle indeed

62. *Metaphysics*, XII, 1071 *b* 3f.
63. *Timaeus*, 28 *b* and 49 *b*.
64. Ibid., 38 *b*.

believed the world to be eternal and refers, in the same context, to al-Fārābi's reproach to Galen, who is known to have suspended judgment on this question.[65]

In Latin Scholastic circles, as illustrated by the example of St. Thomas Aquinas (d. 1274), this interpretation of Maimonides, with its roots in al-Fārābi's *Reconciliation of the Two Sages*, became the official interpretation. In view of Aristotle's uncertainty, or rather his alleged vacillation on the question of whether the world is eternal or not, it was argued, recourse must be had to revelation or the Bible[66] or, as Maimonides put it, to the authority of 'our father Abraham and our teacher Moses'.

On the remaining questions with which the *Reconciliation of the Two Sages* deals, such as the question of vision, Plato and Aristotle, al-Fārābi argues, were in agreement. For, whereas Aristotle held that vision is an affection of sight, Plato held that it consists in an effluence emanating from the eye and meeting the object of vision. A fair appraisal of the two views would reveal that they are not as irreconcilable as appears at first sight; but, according to al-Fārābi, owe to the subtlety of the question and the inadequacy of the language used to describe it with precision.

Similarly, with respect to the alleged divergences of the Two Sages regarding the traits of character and whether they are innate, as Plato states in the *Republic*, or a matter of habituation, as Aristotle states in the *Nicomachean Ethics* (*Niqumāchia*), their divergence is not real, but imagined. For Aristotle in his *Nicomachean Ethics* is talking about transitory 'civil rules of conduct', rather than traits of character which are unalterable; whereas Plato is talking about the traits of character pertaining to the agents and patients of political institutions, which are far less susceptible of change.[67]

With the nature of the soul, its aptitude to receive knowledge and its destiny, the views of the Two Sages are equally reconcilable. Plato's view, given in the *Phaedo*, that knowledge is recollection, is not different, according to al-Fārābi, from Aristotle's view given in *Analytica Posteriora* (*Kitāb al-Burhān*) to the effect that all teaching and all learning rest

65. Cf. *Dālālat al-Hā'irīn*, I, 73, p. 315. (*Guide of the Perplexed*, p. 290).
66. Cf. *Summa Theologica*, I, Q. 46 and 142.
67. *Al-Jam'*, p. 17.

ultimately on pre-existing knowledge, since in both cases knowledge of the particular depends on the pre-existing knowledge of the universal.

As for the destiny of the soul after departing the body, Plato is said by some interpreters to have asserted its immortality, little appreciating that he was in fact reporting Socrates' view of a subtle matter expressed in terms of symbols or indications, rather than conclusive proof. Aristotle, on the other hand, in asserting that all knowledge rests on pre-existing knowledge, as mentioned above, presupposes the soul's pre-existence.[68] Al-Fārābi supports this interpretation by quoting the spurious *Uthulugia*, where it is stated that, in the words of the writer (i.e. Plotinus), 'Sometimes I am often alone with my soul, having been stripped of my body and become an immaterial substance ... Thereupon I am able to see so much beauty and splendor in myself, so long as I wonder, and thus I know that I am a small part of the noble world.' From this noble world of Ideas, Plotinus states, he is able to ascend to the higher divine world.[69]

Thus, the introduction of the pseudo *Theologia Aristotelis* enables al-Fārābi to reconcile Plato and Aristotle on one of the most crucial issues dividing them; namely, the status of the Ideas or Forms, as well as the pre-existence of the soul. He nevertheless goes on to mention rightly that in his *Book of Letters* (as the *Metaphysics* was sometimes called in Arabic), Aristotle did in fact criticize vehemently the view of those who believe in the Ideas or Forms, existing in the 'divine world'. Al-Fārābi then adds, without being aware of the contradiction, that Aristotle affirms 'spiritual forms' in the *Book of Divinity* (i.e. the pseudo Theologia) and declares that they exist in the 'world of divinity'.[70]

To resolve this contradiction, al-Fārābi then proposes three alternatives: 1) the first is that Aristotle contradicted himself; 2) the second is that some of these conflicting statements given in the two books are not his; and 3) the third is that the contradiction is purely apparent, not real. The first alternative is then discounted on the ground that Aristotle was 'too smart and vigilant' to contradict himself in this 'divine science'; the second on the ground that it is too far-fetched to assume that some of the

68. Ibid., p. 20.
69. Ibid., p. 31.
70. Ibid., p. 28.

mentioned books are spurious,[71] given that when they are too famous to be so described. The only alternative left is that they must admit of an interpretation that removes the contradictions in question.

The interpretation proposed by al-Fārābi is ingenious, but does not remove the textual difficulties involved. First, he argues, insofar as God Almighty is a living Creator of this world, and everything in it, 'He must possess in Himself forms of whatever He wishes to create.'[72] This is dictated by the fact that were there no forms or images in the 'essence of the living and willing Creator', we would be compelled to suppose that the world was created haphazardly and purposelessly, which is one of the most repugnant suppositions. Al-Fārābi then proceeds to explain away Plato's use of the terms 'divine world', the 'world of the soul' and the 'world of reason' in the *Timaeus*, as purely figurative. When Plato speaks of higher and lower, as applied to these worlds, he simply means nobler and more honorable, and by the term 'world' in these cases he simply means the locus (*hayyiz, makān*).[73]

A subsidiary strategem used by al-Fārābi in supporting this thesis is the linguistic or semantic one. Philosophers, he says, are forced to use symbolic or figurative language in talking about such noble themes, because of their subtlety. Accordingly, their statements regarding the soul, reason and the divine world, as well as (Plato's) references to the soul's release from the body, which is its prison, so as to rejoin its original abode in the higher world, should not be understood literally.

Finally, with respect to reward and punishment, Aristotle, we are told, did not deny their existence in the realm of nature, and he implicitly believed in them after death, as we can infer from the letter of condolences he wrote to Alexander's mother after his death, in these words: 'As for the witnesses of God in His world, who are the learned souls, they are unanimous that Alexander the Great was one of the most virtuous ... O, mother of Alexander, if you are afraid for Alexander the Great, do not do what draws you apart, or bring upon you that which will stand between you on the Day of Encounter and the band of the

71. *Manhūl* (my reading).
72. Ibid., p. 29.
73. Ibid., p. 30.

righteous; but take care to do what brings you closer to him. The first such action is to attend by your pure self to the matter of offerings in the temple of Zeus [*Diyus*]'.[74] All this, al-Fārābi concludes, proves conclusively that Aristotle believed in punishment and reward, as indeed in life after death.

74. Ibid., p. 32. The above letter has not been preserved in the Greek or Arabic sources known to us. Al-Fārābi must have derived it from some late apocryphal, Neoplatonic source.

3

The Classification of the Sciences

The interrelation of the sciences

To illustrate further al-Fārābi's grasp of the Greek legacy, especially in its Aristotelian dimension, it is worthwhile examining his account of the philosophical, linguistic, theological and juridical sciences given in one of his major writings, the *Enumeration of the Sciences* (*Iḥṣā' al-'Ulūm*).

In the preface of this book, al-Fārābi states that his purpose is to list the various sciences and give their divisions in accordance with a didactic method, best suited for the acquisition of each one of them and the right order in which they should be studied.

The first division is that of the linguistic sciences, which deal either: a) with words and their connotations in any given language as used by some nation or other, or b) with the rules governing the uses of those words.

The linguistic sciences, he adds, include seven subdivisions, called by al-Fārābi in succession: 1) the science of single terms; 2) the science of compound expressions; 3) the science of the laws of single terms; 4) the science of the laws of compound expressions; 5) the science of orthography; 6) the science of locution; and 7) the science of prosody or versification.[1]

1. *Iḥṣā' al-'Ulūm*, p. 59.

This list is followed by a brief account of the subject-matter of these seven subdivisions of the linguistic sciences, the transmission of the terms used by each nation and the literary heritage created by each nation's orators, poets, and men of eloquence. Al-Fārābi then makes some perceptive comments on the remaining subdivisions, which are of casual interest to us.

Logic and mathematics

The second division is that of the philosophical sciences. This division reflects the influence of the Aristotelian syllabus, of which al-Kindi had already given a sketchy and eclectical example in his *Quantity of Aristotle's Writings* (*Kammiyat Kutūb Arisṭuṭalīs*).[2] Al-Fārābi's classification, by contrast, is thorough and systematic. It begins with logic, which he defines as the art that 'lays down the general laws which set the mind straight and guide man toward the path of truth and the right in all those intelligibles wherein he is liable to error'.[3] Logic, al-Fārābi goes on to state, has a certain analogy to grammar, insofar as logic gives us the rules governing intelligibles (*ma'qūlāt*) in the same way that grammar gives us the rules governing terms or expressions. He is careful to note, however, that there are major differences between the two and criticizes those who claim that the study of logic is superfluous, since, like grammar, it may be mastered by practicing logical reasoning, just as one might master grammar by memorizing eloquently literary or poetic discourses.[4]

The subdivisions of logic are then given in accordance with the Arabic and Syriac tradition as eight, corresponding to the Aristotelian *Organon*, to which in those two traditions the *Rhetorica* and *Poetica* were added. These parts correspond to the three modes of expression – internal, external or a combination of both – as well as the five modes of deduction (*qiyās*): the demonstrative, the dialectical, the sophistical, the rhetorical and the poetical.

Al-Fārābi then lists the eight parts of the *Organon* as follows:

2. Cf. *Rasā'il al-Kindi al-Falsafiyah*, I, pp. 363f.
3. Ibid., p. 67.
4. Ibid., p. 73.

1. The *Categories* (*Maqūlat, Qātiguriās*), which deals with single terms and the rules governing them.
2. *On Intepretation* (*'Ibārah, Bāri Ermeniās*: Greek, *Peri Hermeias*), which deals with propositions or compound expressions.
3. *Prior Analytics* (*Qiyās, Analytica Priora*), which deals with the rules of general discourse.
4. *Posterior Analytics* (*Kitāb al-Burhān, Analytica Posteriora*), which deals with the rules of demonstrative arguments.
5. *Dialectic* (*Mawāḍi Jadaliyah, Topica*), which deals with dialectical arguments or questions and answers.
6. *Sophistics* (*Mughālaṭah, Sophistica*).
7. *Rhetoric* (*Khatābah, Rhetorica*), which deals with rhetorical arguments and the varieties of oratorial and eloquent address.
8. *Poetics* (*Kitāb al-Shi'r, Poetica*), which deals with poetical discourses, their varieties and the rules of poetic versification or prosody.[5]

The science of mathematics (*al-Ta'ālīm*; from the Greek *manthano*, 'learn') consists, according to al-Fārābi, of seven parts: arithmetic, geometry, optics, astronomy, music, dynamics and mechanics. Each of these subdivisions has a theoretical and a practical part, the first dealing with the nature of the subject-matter, the second with its application. Al-Fārābi's most interesting remarks turn on astronomy, which is divided into astrology (*'ilm aḥkām al-nujūm*) and 'mathematical astronomy'. The first, to which he devoted a separate and highly critical treatise entitled *Valid and Invalid Inferences in Astrology* (*Mā Yaṣuḥ wa mā la Yaṣuḥ min 'Ilm Aḥkām al-Nujūm*), is defined as 'knowledge of the way in which the planets serve as portents of future events or indices of much of what exists today or has existed in the past'.[6]

In this critical treatise, al-Fārābi marshals a series of arguments to show that the claims of the astrologers or their prognostications are not always reliable. Events in the world, he argues, are determined either by particular causes, which can be ascertained, or by causes that are purely fortuitous. Now, although it is true that heavenly bodies exert a certain

5. Ibid., p. 89.
6. Ibid., p. 102f.

influence on observable terrestrial events, that influence is of two types. Some effects may be determined through astronomical computations or are referable to such physical factors as proximity to the sun, which is the cause of heating; and some are fortuitous, such as the death of a person at sunset or sunrise. The latter type is not determinable and is not subject to the influence of the heavenly bodies in any way; it is, rather, fortuitous. Now, were there no fortuitous events, whose causes are unknown, he argues, there would be no room left for fear or hope and accordingly there would be no natural order in human relations, whether in religious or political matters. For, but for fear and hope, no one will make provision for the future and no subordinate will obey his superior, nor would God Himself be obeyed. Thus, were one absolutely certain of the future sequence of events, he or she would be a fool to plan for the future.[7]

It is to be observed, argues al-Fārābi, that possible or contingent matters are such that their existence is more likely than their non-existence or vice versa, and cannot for that reason be determined by any deduction. Experience itself may be useful in matters that are possible in most cases; whereas in matters that are possible in fewer cases or are equally possible or not, experience is of no avail.

All natural events or actions, al-Fārābi goes on to argue, are possible or contingent. However, insofar as possible matters are unknown, everything unknown has been called possible by people of limited intelligence, who accordingly were led to seek its causes by recourse to terrestrial or celestial investigations or calculations. It cannot be denied that in certain cases the influence of the heavenly bodies on terrestrial events can be accurately determined, as happens in the case of the sun and its proximity to certain damp places leading to evaporation, cloud-formation and rain, which could cause ill-health or death. However, to assert that such occurrences can be known by recourse to auguries or astronomical calculations is a sign of folly.[8] Influences are actually determinable and depend on the properties and movements of the heavenly bodies, which are unalterable and incorruptible; but to refer those influences to certain conjunctions of the planets is pure conjecture.

7. *Ma Yaṣuḥ wa ma lā Yaṣuḥ*, (Dieterici), p. 106.
8. Ibid., p. 110.

As an example of the extravagant claims of astrologers, al-Fārābi cites the alleged influence of the eclipse of the sun on the death of some king or other. For the eclipse of the sun is due to the interposition of the moon between the sun and the earth, shutting the sun out. Thus, every time the light of the sun is shut out by a cloud a king should die or a grave calamity should happen on earth. This is something, al-Fārābi comments, that the fools find repugnant, let alone the wise.[9]

It cannot be denied, he then goes on to say, that the prognostications and auguries of astrologers sometimes prove to be true, sometimes not. If so, they can only be described as conjectures, probabilities or forms of fortune-telling.

Finally, were astrology a science, why is it, al-Fārābi asks, that the most illustrious among astrologers are the least prone to manage their own affairs in the light of their own prognostications? Consequently, it can only be assumed that their profession of that art is merely a matter of deliberate choice, affectation, profit-seeking or cupidity.[10]

Mathematical astronomy, on the other hand, is the study of the earth and the heavenly bodies with a view to determining: a) their shapes, positions, relations to each other and their relative distances from one another, the earth being entirely immovable; b) their motions and the number of those spherical motions, whether common to all of them or peculiar to each one of them; c) their movements and positions in the zodiac and their effects on such terrestrial phenomena as the eclipse of the sun and the moon, their rising and setting and the like; and d) the divisions of the earth into inhabited and uninhabited regions. This is done with a view to determining their major divisions or zones and the way in which these zones are affected by the universal diurnal motions of the spheres and the succession of day and night.[11]

Physics and metaphysics

The three other subdivisions of mathematics – namely, music, dynamics and mechanics – are then briefly discussed, followed by a much fuller discussion of physics and metaphysics.

9. Ibid., p. 112.
10. Ibid., p. 114.
11. Ibid., pp. 103f.

Physics is defined as the study of 'natural bodies and the accidents which inhere in them; as well as the things from which, by which and for which those bodies and accidents inhering in them arise'.[12]

Next, al-Fārābi divides bodies into natural and artificial; the latter are the product of human art or choice; whereas the former are independent of human art or choice. Both natural and artificial bodies exist for the sake of some good or goal and have an efficient and a material cause, which are known only by means of demonstrative arguments. This is a reference to prime matter and the causes of generation of physical objects, which are subject not to empirical observation, but to rational inference only.

The matters, forms, agents and purposes of the generation of bodies are called the first principles of those bodies, and form the subject-matter of the physical sciences. Those bodies are divisible into: 1) simple bodies, by which al-Fārābi means the four elements of water, fire, air and earth, and 2) compound bodies formed from them, such as animals and plants. It is for this reason that the science of physics is divisible into eight parts, corresponding roughly to Aristotle's eight physical treatises:

1. The first investigates the principles and accidents that simple and compound natural bodies have in common. This is covered in Aristotle's *Physics* (*al-Samā' al-Ṭabi'ī*; *Physike Akroesis*).
2. The second investigates the simple bodies (i.e. the four elements), their number and nature, as well as the fifth element[13] of which the heavens are made up. This is discussed in the first book of the *Heavens and the World* (*De Coelo et Mundo*), as Aristotle's *De Coelo* was called in the Arabic sources. This is followed by the discussion of the elements and their corresponding accidents, in the third and fourth parts of that book.
3. The third studies the generation and corruption of natural bodies, as well as the elements. This is contained in the *Generation and Corruption* (*al-Kawn wa'l-Fasād*).
4. The fourth deals with the principles of accidents and the affections, which pertain to the elements exclusively. This is contained in the first three books of the *Meteorology* (*al-Āthār al-'Ulawiyah*).

12. *Iḥṣā'*, p. 111.
13. That is, ether.

5. The fifth studies the bodies compounded from the simple elements, some being of similar parts (*homoemera*) and some of dissimilar parts (i.e. organic) and made up of the former, such as flesh and bone. This is contained in the fourth book of the *Meteorology.*
6. The sixth studies the types of bodies made up of similar parts (i.e. inorganic), such as minerals and stones, and is contained in the *Book of Minerals.*[14]
7. The seventh deals with the varieties of plants, made up of dissimilar parts, and is contained in the *Book of Plants.*[15]
8. The eighth deals with what animals have in common and is contained in the *Book of Animals* and *De Anima.*

By the last statement, al-Fārābi clearly intends the principle of life common to all animals and humans.[16] Nineteen zoological treatises were attributed to Aristotle in the Arabic tradition under the rubric of the *Book of Animals.* Psychology, which for him formed part of the natural sciences, is actually contained in *De Anima* (*Kitāb al-Nafs*) and the *Parva Naturalia*, known in Arabic as *Kitāb al-Hiss wa'l-Mahsūs* (*Sense and Sensibles*).

Having concluded the discussion of the physical corpus, al-Fārābi turns next to metaphysics or the 'divine science' (*al-'Ilm al-Ilāhī*). This science, we are told, is contained in its entirety in Aristotle's book known as the *Metaphysics* (*Mā Ba'd al-Tabī'ah, Metaphysica*). The 'divine science', he goes on to say, is divided into three parts:

1. The first part studies existing entities insofar as they exist. (We may call this part ontology, dealt with in Aristotle's *Metaphysics*, Book VII.)
2. The second deals with the first principles of demonstration of particular sciences, such as the principles of logic, mathematics and physics and stating them correctly, while enumerating the false opinions entertained by the ancients, with respect to these first principles. We might call this part metaphysical epistemology. (Aristotle dealt with these questions and refuted the views of the

14. No such book is given in the ancient lists of Aristotle's works.
15. The extant *De Plantis* in the Aristotelian corpus is a Greek translation of a Latin translation of the Arabic *Kitāb al-Nabāt*, attributed to Nicolaus of Damascus, a late commentator on Aristotle. Cf. W.D. Ross, *Aristotle*, p. 12.
16. *Iḥṣā'*, p. 119.

Sophists, who questioned the possibility of knowledge altogether, in the *Metaphysics*, Book IV.)

3. The third deals with immaterial entities and investigates whether they exist or not, whether they are many or not and whether they are finite or infinite, and shows that they exist, are many and are finite. Al-Fārābi then proceeds to consider whether they are of varying degrees of perfection 'arising from the most imperfect to the more perfect, until they reach at the end, a perfect (being), nothing more perfect than which exists. Nor could there be anything else equal in existence to it. It has no peer and no opposite. This is the First, before which nothing exists, the Prior (being) nothing more prior than which could exist, and the Being who could not have received its being from anything else.'[17] For it is, he concludes, the One that is absolutely first and absolutely the most prior.

In this characterization of the Supreme Being, al-Fārābi goes well beyond Aristotle in the direction of Plato and Plotinus, and formulates in the process the nearest thing to the ontological argument first proposed by St. Anselm (d. 911) and revived in modern times by Descartes (d. 1650).[18]

Al-Fārābi pursues this Platonic–Plotinian line of thought, which is on the whole alien to Aristotle's purpose in *Metaphysics*, Book *XII*, and comments on the way in which this First Being imparts existence, unity and truth to everything else. Being more worthy of the attributes of unity, being and truth than anything else, such a Being must be regarded as identical with God Almighty.

Al-Fārābi then gives, along essentially Plotinian lines also, an account of how existing entities have derived their being from God, how they are ordered and how all His actions are entirely free from injustice, contradiction, imperfection or evil. He finally credits Aristotle, by whom he obviously meant Plotinus, author of the spurious *Uthulūgia*, with the rebuttal of all those false opinions which have imputed imperfection to God's actions and creations. This is done by means of 'demonstrations,

17. Ibid., p. 121. Cf. *Fusūl*, p. 53.
18. See M. Fakhry, 'The Ontological Argument in the Arabic Tradition, the Case of al-Fārābi', *Studia Islamica*, 64, 1986, pp. 5–17.

which yield certain knowledge, regarding which no uncertainty or doubt can occur to any man'.[19]

Ethics and politics

Al-Fārābi concludes the Greek syllabus with a discussion of politics with its two subdivisions, ethics or the study of ethical traits, and politics or the study of political institutions. What the two have in common is the investigation of moral traits and the laws (*sunan*) that ensure that true happiness is attained. To achieve that goal a 'royal rule' is needed in order to safeguard such happiness and the means leading to it.

This royal rule (*ri'āsah malikiyah*) is of two types: the virtuous, which safeguards those moral traits conducive to true happiness, and the non-virtuous, which stresses those actions or traits of character conducive to imaginary happiness. If the aim taught by the royal art is wealth, the rule is called ignominy (*nadhālah*); if honor it is called timocracy (*karanah*); if conquest (*taghallub*) it is called tyranny or despotism, as al-Fārābi calls, along Platonic lines, the four forms of government into which the perfect or 'virtuous' state actually degenerates, as we will see in Chapter 8.

It is significant that in his classification of the practical sciences in *The Enumeration* (*Iḥṣā' al-'Ulūm*), al-Fārābi concentrates almost exclusively on politics, with the barest reference to the other subdivision of the practical sciences, i.e. ethics. This is particularly surprising, since, as mentioned earlier, he was conversant with Aristotle's *Nicomachean Ethics* (*Niqumakhia*), on which he is known to have written a commentary, which is lost, but not with the *Politics*. That famous treatise is the only major work of Aristotle which was never translated into Arabic, for some unknown reason, until modern times. In his *Selected Excerpts* (*Fuṣūl*), it is true, al-Fārābi discusses certain ethical questions, which will be examined later.

Be this as it may, he goes on in the *Enumeration* to argue that politics, like medicine, has two aspects, the enactment of universal laws, on the one hand, and the practical exercise, reinforced by prolonged observation and experience, of those skills which are bound to enable the ruler to deal with particular situations or problems. That is why the political art is divided

19. Ibid., p. 123.

into two parts: a) a legislative part, which lays down the universal rules and precepts, and b) a practical part, which is left to the discretion of the ruler.[20]

The Islamic sciences

The *Enumeration of the Sciences* closes with the two Islamic sciences of jurisprudence (*fiqh*) and theology (*kalām*). The first is defined as the art whereby 'one is able to deduce, from what the lawgiver (i.e. the Prophet) has explicitly stated, the determination, in specific cases, of that which he did not state explicitly'.[21] This should be done in light of the intent of the lawgiver, who has legislated for a given nation and a given religion (*millah*). For in each religion, we find certain beliefs, which include beliefs in God, His attributes, the creation of the world and such like, on the one hand, and certain rituals that glorify God and regulate various transactions, on the other. That is why jurisprudence has two parts, a part bearing on beliefs and another on actions, known traditionally as the part dealing with fundamentals (*uṣūl*) and that dealing with particulars (*furū'*).

Theology is then defined as the art whereby one is able to 'support specific beliefs and practices, which the lawgiver has enunciated explicitly, as well as the rebuttal of all contrary statements'.[22] Like jurisprudence, theology has two parts, one bearing on beliefs, and the other on actions. Although the two are different insofar as the theologian does not make any deductions from the explicit statements of the lawgiver, as the jurist does, the theologian actually uses the same principles from which jurists make their deductions in support of the beliefs handed down by the lawgiver; i.e. the religious or sacred texts embodied in the Qur'an and the Traditions of the Prophet (*Ḥadīth*).

As regards the ways in which the various religions should be supported, a group of Mutakallimun, by whom al-Fārābi probably meant the literalists or traditionalists, have held that religious beliefs and precepts should not be tested by recourse to human judgment or reasoning, 'because they are higher than them, since they derive from

20. Ibid., p. 127.
21. Ibid., p. 130. Cf. Kitāb al-Millah, p. 50.
22. Ibid., p. 131. Cf. Kitāb al-Millah, pp. 47f.

divine revelation and contain certain divine mysteries which human reasons cannot circumscribe or grasp'.[23]

Moreover, this group has argued that the whole function of revelation is specifically to impart to humankind that which cannot be circumscribed by reason; otherwise this revelation would be entirely superfluous, in which case there would be no need for prophethood or revelation. Sometimes what religion imparts to humankind in the form of cognitions that are inaccessible to human reason is rejected as rationally repugnant, although they are perfectly sound, for 'divine intellects'. Moreover, no matter what degree of human perfection a man may have attained, his position in the eyes of the people of 'divine intellects' is no better than that of a child or a dumb person. It follows that what has been revealed by God is perfectly sound and should not be questioned. In support of this claim, the advocates of the veracity of revealed truth invoke the miracles that are performed by a prophet, or the testimony of preceding scholars of undoubted veracity. Hence, there is no need for reasoning, speculation, deliberation or theorizing in confirmation of their reports.[24]

A second group, by whom al-Fārābi probably meant the Mu'tazilites, hold that religion should be defended by recourse to the explicit statements or words of the founder of religion (i.e. the Prophet), on the one hand, and by appeal to sensible, generally accepted rational principles. Whatever is found to support religious teaching, however remotely, should be invoked in defense of the position they have adopted. Should it appear that some of these principles are in conflict with that teaching, it will be necessary to interpret the words of the founder of religion (i.e. Prophetic Traditions or *Ḥadith*) in such a way as to conform with the above principles; or conversely to manipulate (*yuzayyaf*) those principles which are in conflict with religious teaching. Where those principles are in conflict with each other, the right course is to choose those which are in conformity with religious teaching and overlook the rest. If none of those devices proves to be adequate, this group will simply resort to the same position as the first group and declare dogmatically that

23. Ibid., p. 132.
24. Ibid., p. 135. The reference here is to the authority of the Companions of the Prophet (*Sahābah*) or their successors (*Tābiūn*).

the religious propositions or precepts they believe in are true and incorrigible, because they were enunciated by one (i.e. the Prophet) who could not lie or err.[25]

A third group, we are then told by al-Fārābi, have recommended another strategem, consisting in defending repugnant aspects of their religion, by drawing attention to those equally repugnant aspects of other religions. This is, of course, a common 'apologetic' strategem, which is not restricted to any one historical group, Muslim or other.

A fourth group, having become convinced that none of the above means of persuasion or rational discourse is sufficient to silence the opponent, are willing to use other means, such as intimidating, threatening or confounding the opponent, to achieve their goals.[26]

Finally, a fifth group is mentioned as taking a more aggressive line. Since for them their religion is true and unquestionable, they feel justified in dispelling any doubts regarding it and repelling the attacks of their opponents in any way possible. They will not hesitate in these circumstances to resort to downright lying, sophistry, stupefaction (*baht*) or hyperbole. The opponents of their religion, they are convinced, are either: 1) declared enemies with whom recourse to lying and sophistry is permissible, as happens in holy war (*jihād*), or 2) not real enemies, but people who are deficient in intelligence or sound judgment. 'It is permissible that such persons may be prevailed upon, by recourse to lying or sophistry, as is done in dealing with women and small boys.'[27]

It is, perhaps, out of a Shi'ite sense of dissimulation (*taqiyah*), that al-Fārābi refrains from naming any historical representatives of any of the five groups. The first group appears to refer to Hanbalites or Malikites, who had no use for argument whatsoever; the second to the Mu'tazilites, who were celebrated advocates of interpretation; the third to ordinary apologists, who usually tend to counter fault with fault; the fourth and fifth to supporters of the established religious order, who believe themselves justified in exploiting their authority to achieve their dialectical aims, by any means, including open warfare.

25. Ibid., p. 136.
26. Ibid., p. 137.
27. Ibid., p. 138.

4

Al-Fārābi as Logician

The logical corpus

Of the three areas in which al-Fārābi excelled – logic, politics and metaphysics – it was in the first area that he made a significant historical contribution. At a time when Syriac-speaking logicians, whether Nestorian or Jacobite, had stopped short, apparently for religious reasons, of pursuing the logical inquiry beyond the first preliminary books of Aristotelian logic – the *Categories*, the *Interpretation*, *Analytica Priora* and the *Isagoge* of Porphyry – as we have seen, al-Fārābi was willing to pursue this inquiry to the limit. In fact, al-Fārābi is known to have paraphrased or commented on all the parts of the Aristotelian logical corpus, known as the *Organon*, together with the *Isagoge* of Porphyry and the *Rhetorica* and *Poetica* of Aristotle.[1]

The publication of al-Fārābi's logical writings starting in the 1950s has confirmed the above assessment. The collection starts with a series of introductory treatises, in which al-Fārābi engages in the analysis of logical terms in a manner that was unmatched until modern times. This series includes the *Terms Used in Logic* (*al-Alfāz al-Musta'malah fi'l-Manṭiq*),

1. See Bibliography. Of the early Greek commentaries, Ammonius, Simplicius, and David the Armenian included the *Rhetorica* and the *Poetica* in the *Organon*, while Alexander of Aphrodisias excluded them. Cf. Madkour, *L'Organon d'Aristote dans le monde Arabe*, p. 13.

the *Introductory Treatise* (*Kitāb al-Tawṭi'ah*), the *Five Sections* (*al-Fuṣūl al-Khamsah*), the *Introduction* (or *Isāghugī*) and the *Categories* (*al-Maqūlāt*).

To these introductory treatises should be added the large commentary on *De interpretatione* (*Kitāb al-'Ibārah*; *Peri hermeneias*), the paraphrases of *Analytica Priora* (*Kitāb al-Qiyās*), the *Analytical Treatise* (*Kitāb al-Taḥlīl*), the *Analytica Posteriora* (*Kitāb al-Burhān*), *Sophistica* and *Topica*. These are followed by the paraphrases of *Rhetorica* and *Poetica*, which formed part of the *Organon* in the Arabic and Syriac traditions, as already mentioned. Al-Fārābi is reported in the ancient sources to have written commentaries or glosses on *Analytica Priora*, *Analytica Posteriora*, the *Categories* and the *Isagoge* that have not survived.[2]

The analysis of logical terms

Perhaps al-Fārābi's most original contribution to the study of logic, as already mentioned, was his analysis of logical terms. In the *Five Sections in Logic*, he has given us a methodical analysis of a series of technical terms used by logicians, including deduction, prior, noun, verb, article and 'to be'. In the *Terms Used in Logic*, he lists the variety of terms that 'We have received from those proficient in the grammar of the people who speak the Greek language',[3] of which some are relevant to the study of logic, according to him. These include such terms as pronoun, definite article, copula, and negative and positive particles. He then proceeds to argue that, since the aim of logicians is to determine the existence, quantity, time and quality of a given entity or action, they will need to borrow from the grammarians the appropriate terms. Thus, they will use such terms as: 'what', to determine the existence of the object, and 'how', 'which' and 'why' to determine, respectively, the modality, the type of the thing and the reason why it is what it is.[4] Apart from these terms common to logic and grammar, al-Fārābi engages next in a discussion of the relation of grammar to logic. He argues that the aim of the grammarian is to determine the relation of terms (*al-fāz*) according to

2. See Ibn Abī 'Usaybi'ah, *Uyūn al-Anbā'*, *I*, p. 609.
3. *Al-Alfāz al-Musta'malah*, p. 42.
4. Ibid., pp. 53f.

the rules of composition (*tarkīb*); whereas the aim of the logician is to determine the relation of concepts (*ma'āni*) according to the rules of predication (*ḥaml*).

It is of some historical interest to dwell briefly on the controversy that raged around the relation of grammar to logic during the tenth century and beyond, in Arab-Islamic circles. A memorable debate between Abū Bishr Mattā, one of al-Fārābi's teachers and a leading logician of Baghdad, and Abū Sa'īd al-Sirāfi, a grammarian and jurist of some standing, in the presence of the vizier Ibn al-Furāt, in the year 932 in Baghdad, reported by Abu-Hayyān al-Tawhidi (d. 1024).

Abū Bishr Mattā, we are told, argued that logic is a tool for distinguishing incorrect from correct speech (*kalām ṣaḥīḥ*), to which al-Sirāfi responded that surely that distinction is a prerogative of grammar. How else could logic, invented by a Greek (i.e. Aristotle), he then asks, guard a Turk, an Indian or an Arab against incorrect speech? Mattā's answer, reminiscent of al-Fārābi's, is that logic is concerned with concepts underlying linguistic usage, wherein grammatical and national conventions are irrelevant to the truth or falsity of statements made in any given language.[5]

The discussion of predication in logic leads al-Fārābi to the discussion of universals, which include genus, species, as well as accidents and differentiae. This is followed by a discussion of the conventional modes of logical discourse; namely, deduction (*qiyās*), demonstration (*burhān*) and sophistry (*mughālaṭah*), to which is later added dialectic (*jadal*).[6]

In the *Book of Letters*, al-Fārābi discusses terms that are common to philosophy in general and logic in particular. These terms include 'that' (*anna*), 'being' (*mawjūd*), 'concept', 'relation', 'substance' (*jawhar*), 'self' (*dhāt*) and 'thing'. Of these terms, 'being' is the most fundamental, since it is common to the ten categories and is applied analogically to all that is. In general, it is used in three senses: a) as a predicate of all the categories; b) as a synonym of the true; or c) as denoting any essence existing outside the soul (which corresponds to its Platonic use as a predicate of the Ideas). The fourth use of 'being' is the copulative sense, which corresponds to the

5. Cf. al-Tawhīdi, *al-Imta' wa'l-Mu'ānasah*, p. 111.
6. Cf. *al-Alfāz al-Musta'malah*, p. 107. Cf. Aristotle, *Topica*, 100 *a* and *Sophistica*, 165 *b*.

Greek term *estin*, the Persian term *hast* and the Soghdian term *esti*, as al-Fārābi explains.[7]

'Substance' or 'entity' (*jawhar*) is equally fundamental and is used in a number of senses: 1) to denote the individual that is not present in a subject;[8] 2) any predicate denoting what that individual is; and 3) whatever defines the essence of a given species (i.e. secondary substance). The most general meaning of 'substance' is then given as that which defines the essence of anything belonging to any of the nine categories, which depend on substance, although substance itself does not depend on any of them. Here, al-Fārābi comments on the etymology of the term *jawhar*, meaning 'jewel' in Persian, and suggests that this term was applied to the category of substance because it is the most precious.[9] Aristotle, we are then told, calls the individual which is not in a subject the primary substance and the species or genus (i.e. the universal) secondary substances.[10] He finally refers to the other use of the term 'substance' as that which is equivalent to the essence or quiddity (*māhiyah*) of the thing.[11]

Other terms discussed in the *Book of Letters* are interrogatory terms, which include 'what', 'who', 'whether', 'why', 'how', 'how much', 'where' and 'when'. Some of these terms, we are told, such as 'where', 'when', 'how' and 'how much' belong to the class of the well-known categories of place, time, quality and quantity. Others inquire whether the existent (*mawjūd*) exists, why, and what it is, as discussed in the opening parts of Aristotle's *Analytica Posteriora*. These terms are used to inquire, once the existence of the object is ascertained, what its cause is, as when we ask why (*limādha*) it exists; or its definition, as when we ask 'what' (*mādha*), which is also one of the causes of the existent (i.e. the formal cause); whereas the question 'by what?' (*bimādha*) refers to its efficient cause.[12] He then goes on to comment on the variety of uses of these terms in the different logical contexts, i.e.

7. Cf. *Kitāb al-Ḥurūf*, p. 111.
8. In Aristotle's *Categories*, 2 *a* 10, 'substance' (*ousia*) in the primary sense is defined as that which is not predicable of a subject, nor present in a subject; i.e. the individual, who is the subject of all predications.
9. Cf. *Kitāb al-Ḥurūf*, pp. 101, 97f.
10. Ibid., p. 102. Aristotle, *Categories*, 2 *b* 7.
11. Ibid., p. 105.
12. Cf. Ibid., pp. 204f.

the scientific (or philosophical), the dialectical, the sophistical and the rhetorical, but overlooks, for some reason, the poetical.

Of the philosophical uses, mathematics seeks to determine what the thing actually is, by asking what it is; whereas in physics, its agent and purpose are sought, by asking, 'Does it exist and how?' The same is true of politics (*'ilm madani*), according to al-Fārābi. In metaphysics, on the other hand, we seek to determine the agent, the essence and the purpose of 'divine things', by asking, 'Do they exist or not?' Once the answer is yes, we then proceed to ask, 'How they are and through what they came to be [*bimādha*]?'

Here, al-Fārābi raises an intriguing question. When we ask 'Does God exist?', do we mean that His existence outside the soul corresponds to His existence in the soul, or not? And if the former, then how and by what is He caused? These last three questions, however, do not apply to God, since, unlike everything else, He has no cause, either material, formal or final. The only sense in which we can ask: 'Does He exist?' (*hal*), is simply whether He is a substantive entity (*dhāt*) or not.[13] The implication appears to be that once we have determined that God exists, as an entity (*dhāt*), we are no longer supposed to ask any other question, since, as al-Fārābi argues in the *Virtuous City*, God as the First (Being) has no definition, no opposite, no form, no matter and no purpose (*ghāyah*).[14]

In the *Introductory Risālah*, al-Fārābi discusses more traditional logical terms, such as predicates, whether simple or compound, substance, differentia (*faṣl*) and property (*khāṣṣah*). Simple universal predicates are then given as five, along the lines of Porphyry's *Isagoge*; namely, genus, species, differentia, property and accident,[15] with which he also deals in his own *Isagoge* or *Introduction* (*al-Madkhal*). In that treatise, he departs somewhat from Porphyry's procedure by including a section on 'compound universals', as he calls them, which include definition (*ḥadd*) and description (*rasm*). Definition, he writes, is a universal compound made up of a genus and differentia. Where the definition has more than one differentia, the specific one is to be chosen, and where more than one,

13. Ibid., p. 218.
14. Cf. *Al-Madinah al-Fāḍilah*, pp. 23f.
15. *Risālah fi'l-Tawṭi'ah* in *Islamic Quarterly*, 2, 1955, p. 228f.

the lowest, or *infima species*, as it is called in Aristotelian logic. Description, on the other hand, is a statement of what a thing is by reference to accidental rather than essential differentiae. An example of definition is 'Man is a rational animal'; of a description, 'Man is a laughing animal.'[16]

The demonstrative art

We have already referred to al-Fārābi's view of the relation of logic to grammar, as mentioned in the *Enumeration of the Sciences*. In the *Introductory Risālah*, a more detailed account of this relation is given, in the context of the discussion of the scope of logic.

He begins by distinguishing the two varieties of the sciences, analytical or deductive (*qiyāsiyah*) and non-analytical. He defines the former as those sciences which are essentially theoretical, including philosophy proper, dialectic, sophistry, rhetoric and poetics, as against those sciences which are essentially practical, including medicine, carpentry, construction, architecture and the like. Sometimes, it is true, he argues, that these practical sciences or arts resort to theoretical methods of proof, but only incidentally. Philosophy, on the other hand, always uses the analytical or deductive method. This method has five subdivisions: 1) the demonstrative (*burhāniyah*), in which the truth is sought and communicated in all matters that admit of certainty; 2) the dialectical (*jadaliyah*), in which persuasion is sought regarding generally accepted principles (*mashhūrāt*); 3) the sophistical, where the aim of the speaker is persuasion by recourse to questionable principles (its aim is essentially deception [*tamwīh*] or trickery) – in this mode of discourse, the speaker aims to give the impression that he or she is in possession of wisdom, but this is not the case; 4) the rhetorical method aims at persuading the hearer by securing his or her assent as devoid of certainty; 5) the poetical aims at simulation or mimicry (*muhākāt*, *mimesis*), by recourse to what is similar in words, just as sculpture is a form of simulation by recourse to material figures or solids.

After listing the eight logical treatises, of Aristotle's *Organon*, al-Fārābi concludes by stating that logic is a tool (*ālah*) which, used properly, will yield certainty (*yaqīn*) in all the theoretical and practical

16. Cf. Isāghugi aw al-Madkhal, "Al-Fārābi's Eisagoge," *Islamic Quarterly*, 3, 1956, p. 127.

sciences and is absolutely indispensable for attaining that goal. Its name, *manṭiq*, he says, derives from speech (*nuṭq*),[17] which the ancient philosophers divided into two parts: a) the power to conceive of intelligibles in both the practical and theoretical fields (this they called 'inward speech'); b) the power of 'outer speech' or expression in spoken language.[18]

The discussion of the demonstrative methods of proof is the subject-matter of Aristotle's *Analytica Posteriora*, of which al-Fārābi has written a paraphrase, entitled *Kitāb al-Burhān* (*Book of Demonstration*). Here, he begins by dividing all modes of discourse in the traditional Arab manner, which has probably a Stoic basis, into conception (*taṣawwur*) and assent (*taṣdīq*), corresponding roughly to definition and judgment. This is followed by a discussion of the varieties of assent: demonstrative, dialectical and rhetorical.

In his discussion of the demonstrative mode of assent, regarded by Aristotle as the highest such mode, al-Fārābi distinguishes between the knowledge of the fact (*oti*) and the cause of the fact (*dioti*), along essentially Aristotelian lines.[19] The fact, according to him, is known directly, through either sense-experience, external evidence or proof (*dalīl*). Once the fact is known, we are led to seek its causes, by one of the three methods mentioned above. These causes are then given as the material, the formal, the efficient and the final. Of these, the knowledge of the formal and the final entails the knowledge of the thing necessarily; that of the material and the efficient entails simply that the thing may exist as possible or probable.

The complete knowledge of an entity is the knowledge of both its proximate and ultimate causes. Thus, in explaining the eclipse of the moon, it is not enough to say that the moon is in the center of the ecliptic, which is the ultimate cause of the eclipse, but we should add, as its proximate cause, the interposition of the earth between the sun and the moon, thus concealing the light of the sun.[20]

17. Compare the Greek *lego*, 'I speak', and *logiky*, or 'logic'.
18. Cf. *Risālah fi'l-Tawti'ah*, in *Islamic Quarterly*, 2, 1955, p. 228.
19. Cf. *Kitāb al-Burhān*, pp. 26f. Cf. *Analytica Posteriora*, I, 78 *a* 22.
20. Ibid., p. 43.

Demonstrative syllogisms, which lead to certain knowledge (*'ilm*, *episteme*), differ from other types of syllogisms insofar as their premises are necessary and prior to the conclusion. Once these premises are posited, the conclusion will follow necessarily. Some sciences, such as mathematics and physics, deal with particular entities or principles, such as motion or magnitude. Metaphysics, on the other hand, deals with universal entities or principles, insofar as they lead to those ultimate principles which are common to all things, such as being, formal and final causes, etc.[21]

Like Aristotle, in the *Analytica Posteriora*, al-Fārābi deals in the second part of *Kitāb al-Burhān* with definition, its rules and its relation to demonstration. He begins by positing as a premise that a definition consists of a single term or a phrase, which may be used as the conclusion or premise of a demonstration. For instance, if we define thunder as a sound caused by a cloud (or rather the collision of two clouds), then add 'involving rippling in the cloud', we would get the following syllogism:

> This cloud is accompanied by a rippling wind;
> Now, this wind causes a sound;
> Therefore, the cloud causes a sound.

This kind of syllogism, according to al-Fārābi, may yield a definitional conclusion, in which the terms may be rearranged in such a way as to yield this definition of thunder:

> Thunder is a sound in the cloud due to the rippling of wind in it.

The difference, according to al-Fārābi, is that the terms that were prior in the demonstration – namely, the major premise and the middle term (or cloud and rippling sound) – are relegated to the end in the definition. Thus, what was prior in the demonstration is posterior in the definition.[22]

Definition differs from demonstration insofar as its formula does not entail a judgment, as is the case with demonstration, and thus could be used as part of a judgment. However, a definition involves two parts, one which could be predicated of the *definiendum*, the other not. Thus, if we define a circle as a figure inscribed by a single line and which has a center

21. Ibid., p. 62f.
22. Ibid., p. 47.

from which all the lines drawn to the circumference are equal, the term 'figure' is predicable of a circle, but not a single line. For the circle is not a single line, but is a figure inscribed by a single line, which is actually part of the differentia of a figure defined as a circle.[23] Al-Fārābi concludes from this statement that of the two components of the definition, the genus and the differentia, the genus is integral to the *definiendum*, whereas the differentia is not. Thus, when we define a wall as a body that holds the roof, holding the roof is not an essential part of the concept of the wall. Similarly, if we define the Deity as a being who moves the world, moving the world is not an essential part of the nature of the Deity,[24] to which a variety of differentiae apply.

Of the less conventional methods of definition, al-Fārābi mentions the method of Xenocrates, which consists in defining the object by demonstration, and that of Plato by way of division or dichotomy. The first method presupposes the knowledge of the middle term of the demonstration; the second presupposes the knowledge of the genus under which the *definiendum* is subsumed, as well as the essential differentia determining each of these genera in succession.[25] In other words, both methods involve a petition of principle. In Aristotelian logic, the differentia is known either by induction or by deduction, but not a priori, as the above two methods in a sense presuppose.

Rhetoric and poetics

The other two methods of discourse, the rhetorical and the poetical, differ from the demonstrative in a variety of ways. To begin, whereas the aim of demonstration is certainty (*yaqīn*), that of rhetoric is persuasion (*iqnā'*). Persuasion, al-Fārābi argues in his *Rhetoric* (*Kitāb al-Khātābah*), is a form of conjecture (*ẓann*), in which one believes a thing to be such and such, although it is possible for it to be otherwise.[26] However, conjecture and certainty have in common that they are both species of opinion (*ra'y*), which is liable to truth or falsity. Now, propositions that are the subjects of

23. Ibid., p. 45f.
24. Ibid., p. 48.
25. Cf. Ibid., pp. 52f. Cf. Aristotle, *Analytica Posteriora*, II, 5; *Topica* IV, 1, VI, 1–5.
26. Cf. *Kitāb al-Khātābah*, in *Deux ouvrages inédits*, p. 31.

opinion are either necessary or possible. Necessary propositions, however, are either true absolutely or true at a certain time, in the sense that before that time their existence or non-existence was actually possible. These are called existential propositions.

Certainty pertains exclusively to what is necessary; so that the types of certainty appear to correspond to the two types of necessity; namely, absolute certainty or certainty at all times, and relative certainty, or certainty at a certain time only. Absolute certainty, however, does not involve any possibility whatsoever, unlike the relative certainty of (existential) propositions, which could be attended by both certainty and conjecture, as happens when one is certain of the existence of the object in the present, but not in the future.[27]

Next, al-Fārābi discusses the two meanings of the possible, which is the object of conjecture: a) the unknown whose meaning indicates the existence of the object to be sought, and b) some aspect of the existence of any future occurrences or entities. Thus, the possible associated with conjecture is not the possible as an attribute of what exists outside the soul, but only in relation to us, in other words, subjectively. For instance, when we say that Zayd is standing, our statement is necessary so long as he is standing, although prior to that time the statement was possible.[28]

Doubt (*shakk*), which is the opposite of certainty, is next discussed. It is defined by al-Fārābi as the suspension of judgment with respect to two opinions equally credible. This equality consists in the necessity of what each entails, or the equal possibility of their existence.[29] 'Firm conjecture', on the other hand, consists in thoroughly grasping the subject of a proposition, to the point of silencing the opponent by rhetorical or dialectical methods of discourse. However, al-Fārābi states, the rhetorical method precedes in time the dialectical and is followed by the demonstrative. Thus, the ancients used the rhetorical method, coupled with the sophistical, in theoretical enquiries for a long time, until they discovered the dialectical method; whereupon they rejected the rhetorical method in philosophy and adopted the dialectical. This continued up to

27. Ibid., p. 37.
28. Ibid., p. 37.
29. Ibid., p. 55.

the time of Plato, who was the first to introduce the demonstrative method, and to distinguish it clearly from the other methods – the dialectical, the sophistical, the rhetorical and the poetical. It was Aristotle, however, who laid down the general rules of demonstration, in his *Analytica Posteriora* (*Kitāb al-Burhān*).[30]

From that time on, al-Fārābi continues, philosophers rejected the old methods in theoretical enquiries, reserving the dialectical method for instructing the public and the sophistical for examination or admonition. However, the rhetorical method continued to be used in all the arts, including the instruction of the public in theoretical inquiries and political transactions. Al-Fārābi concedes that, despite its wide-ranging application in all the arts, rhetoric is essentially concerned with seeking to persuade in all matters common to the public. Thus, it could be used to persuade in medical matters, for example, by recourse to what is accessible to the physician and the public at large, rather than to special methods peculiar to the physician.[31]

The broader scope of the rhetorical art is illustrated by al-Fārābi in a variety of ways. Rhetoricians might resort to a dubious tactic in order to disparage their opponents and glorify themselves, as Galen does in attacking his opponents and singing the praises of his own country and his parents.[32] Rhetoricians might also appeal to their hearers' emotions of partisanship and uncontrolled anger or try to win their sympathy by rousing their indignation, sense of compassion or cruelty. Rhetoricians may also appeal to their hearers' sense of moral integrity or affectation, as Galen does in these words, as al-Fārābi reports: 'My statement is best understood, appreciated or approved by the intelligent and truth-loving youth, who is true to his original nature and has not been swayed by false opinions or the like.'[33]

Rhetoricians may also resort to the tactic of either exaggerating the importance of the matter at issue, belittling it or embellishing it, as Sophists and dialecticians also are prone to do; or they might distort the

30. Ibid., p. 55.
31. Ibid., p. 61.
32. Ibid., p. 71. Al-Fārābi refers specifically to Galen's *The Art of Therapy* (*Hīlat al-Bur'*) and the *Opinions of Hippocrates and Plato*, which were well-known in Arabic.
33. Ibid., p. 75. The specific locus of this statement of Galen is not given.

statement of the opponent and dwell on its inadequacy or falsify it in a variety of ways.

Another tactic of rhetoricians is to appeal to the written laws of the community or the testimony of trustworthy witnesses. Al-Fārābi gives as an example of the first tactic Galen's statement that the concupiscent faculty is located in the liver, on the ground that the law (*sunnah*) in his country called for extirpating the liver of the adulterer, or his statement in his *Ethics* that the mind is located in the brain, on the ground that people who regard a person as dumb say, 'He is without a brain'. Galen is also said to have argued that the locus of courage is the heart, on the ground that people refer to the coward as one who has no heart.[34]

After reviewing the traditional rules of deduction or syllogisms, al-Fārābi comments that rhetoricians in general tend to use conditional syllogisms, whether hypothetical or disjunctive, because they are more effective in persuading the public. The argument known as *reductio ad absurdum* (*qiyās al-khulf*) is used mostly in refutations, such as: 'If every man is not sensible, then every animal is not sensible, which is absurd.'[35] He concludes the discussion by giving a definition of the terms 'proof' (*dalīl*), 'sign', 'representation' (*tamthīl*) and the last mentioned term's relation to analogy, which was a favorite method of legal interpretation for the jurists. However, he is critical of this method of analogy, to which the equivocal term *qiyās* is applied by the jurists and the Mutakallimun, on the ground that it is reducible to similarity (*shabah*), rather than deduction in the strict sense, and is a weak form of reasoning, used by the rhetoricians also.[36]

Since the Arabic logical corpus, as we have seen, included both rhetoric and poetics, it was natural that logicians, like al-Fārābi, should undertake the discussion of rhetorical and poetical discourse in conjunction. For they both were believed to belong to the syllogistic art, although they both fall short of the certainty at which demonstration aims. They differ, it was held, however, insofar as rhetoric seeks

34. Ibid., p. 77. The *Ethics* of Galen has survived in Arabic only. As for the locus of the mind, Galen disagreed with Aristotle, who held that it was the heart, as al-Fārābi held too. Cf. *Al-Madīnah al-Fāḍilah*, pp. 74f.
35. Ibid., p. 103.
36. Ibid., pp. 85, 117f.

persuasion, whereas poetics seeks simulation (*muhākāt*, mimesis), by recourse to imaginative representations, which play no part in demonstration. Al-Fārābi claims, however, that poetics has a certain analogy to the science (*'ilm*) sought by the demonstrative art, the conjecture (*ẓann*) sought by the dialectical art and the persuasion (*iqnā'*) sought by the rhetorical art and this justifies, according to him, its inclusion in the syllogistic arts.[37]

In the *Excerpts* (*Fuṣūl*), al-Fārābi explains that the aim of poetry is to 'improve the imaginative representation' of the subject in question. It has six varieties, three of which are commendable and three reprehensible. The former include: a) those forms of poetry which seek to improve the rational faculty, direct its actions and reflections towards happiness, glorify divine matters and goods and represent the virtues as noble and the vices as ignoble. Poetry also includes: b) those forms which seek to moderate the base emotions of anger, arrogance, impudence, cruelty and love of conquest; or c) to moderate the emotions associated with weakness and proclivity to seeking the base pleasures, fear, timidity and love of luxury. The three reprehensible forms of poetry are summarily stated by al-Fārābi as the opposites of the former three. For these corrupt what the former three have reformed and incline the hearer to seek excess rather than moderation. The varieties of tunes and songs, al-Fārābi adds, correspond to the varieties of poetry and its subdivisions.[38] It follows, then, that poetry and song had for al-Fārābi a didactic or moral function, with which most Arab literary critics tended to agree.

As regards the inclusion of poetics in the logical corpus – a view that Arab logicians unanimously subscribed to – it is noteworthy that this view was in sharp contrast to the view of Aristotle in his *Poetics*. Here, he states that the function of the poet 'is to describe, not the thing that has happened, but the kind of thing that might happen; i.e. what is possible as being probable or necessary'.[39] In that sense, the function of the poet is different from that of the historian, he adds, insofar as 'the one describes the thing that has been and the other a kind of thing that might be'.

37. Cf. *Jawāmi' al-Shi'r* (*Appendix Talkhis K. Ariṣṭuṭālis fi al-Shi'r*), p. 172.
38. Cf. *Fusūl*, pp. 64f.
39. *Poetics*, 1451 *b* 2.

Accordingly, poetry is more akin to philosophy than history, Aristotle concludes, insofar as its statements are of the nature of the universal, whereas those of history are of the nature of the particular. Moreover, poetical discourse falls short of apodeictic certainty or truth and falsity with which syllogistic reasoning is concerned and could not for that reason be included in the logical corpus.

5

Theory of Knowledge

The nature of scientific knowledge

Science (*'ilm*) or genuine knowledge is defined in the *Excerpts* (*Fuṣūl*) as the excellence of the theoretical part of the soul whereby 'certainty is achieved within the soul, regarding the existence of those entities which do not depend for their being and subsistence on human production; as well as the determination of what each one of them is and how it is, by recourse to demonstrations consisting of true, necessary, universal and primary premises, securely grasped and naturally known by reason'.[1]

An essential characteristic of this type of knowledge, according to al-Fārābi, is necessity and universality. It must bear on what is unchangeable; for what changes from one state to another, is true today and false tomorrow, cannot be the object of genuine knowledge or certainty. That is why the ancient philosophers excluded the latter type of knowledge from the category of certain knowledge; as distinct from the knowledge of what is unchangeable. An example of the first type: this man is sitting now; an example of the second: there is an odd number.

The highest type of this theoretical knowledge, for al-Fārābi, is wisdom (*ḥikmah*), which is 'the knowledge of the *ultimate* causes of all

1. *Fuṣūl*, p. 51.

existing entities, as well as the *proximate* causes, of everything caused', by which he appears to mean 'first philosophy' or metaphysics and 'second philosophy' or physics, respectively. This double type of knowledge consists 'in knowing that entities exist, what they are, how they are and, if many, how they culminate in an orderly fashion, in a Single Being, who is the cause of those ultimate entities, as well as the lower proximate entities'.[2] Such a Being is the True One, whose subsistence (*qiwām*) does not depend on anything else, being thoroughly self-sufficient. He is, in addition, incorporeal and His being is entirely different from the being of other entities, which do not resemble Him except in name. His other characteristics or attributes will be discussed in Chapter 6.

In contradistinction to theoretical knowledge, practical knowledge is described by al-Fārābi as the domain of practical reason or 'the faculty whereby man acquires, after numerous experiences and prolonged observations of sensible things, certain premises which enable him to determine what ought to be preferred or avoided in those (voluntary) matters which depend on our actions'.[3]

This practical reason is then identified with prudence, *ta'aqqul* or *phronesis*, as Aristotle called it. The aim of prudence is the choice of the best means conducive to happiness or any other intermediate goal conducive to happiness, as the ultimate goal. Its subdivisions are: 1) skill (*kays*), consisting in choosing the best means of attaining any *particular* good; 2) cunning (*dahā'*), which consists in choosing the best means of attaining a *great* good, such as wealth, pleasure or dignity; and 3) malice (*khubth*), which consists in choosing the best means of attaining a *base* goal, such as a base gain or pleasure.

Prudence can take other more general forms. Thus, we may have prudence in the management of the household or the city-state, called by al-Fārābi, respectively, economic (from Greek *oikia*, or 'household') and political prudence. Thus, prudence can take the form of either giving advice to others (*mashūri*), stirring animosity (*khusūmi*) or devising strategems for opposing or repulsing the enemy.[4]

2. Ibid., p. 52.
3. Ibid., p. 54.
4. Ibid., p. 58.

A more systematic account of certain knowledge (*'ilm yaqīni*) is given in al-Fārābi's *Paraphrase of Aristotle's Analytica Posteriora*, known in Arabic as the *Book of Demonstration (Kitāb al-Burhān)*. Here, he states that certain knowledge is threefold: 1) the certainty that the thing exists, or the knowledge *that* the thing is, called the knowledge of existence or the 'knowledge that' (*'ilm anna*); 2) the certain knowledge of the cause of the thing, called the 'knowledge why'; 3) the certain knowledge of both together.[5] The syllogisms (*maqāyīs*) used in attaining this threefold certainty are also three: a) what proves the existence of the thing only; b) what proves its cause only; and c) what proves the two together. That type of syllogism which is made up of necessary and certain premises and yields all three forms of certain knowledge is demonstration (*burhān*).

Al-Fārābi then proceeds to define *demonstration* in the absolute sense, as that which proves the existence and the cause of the thing together. This leads him to the discussion of the Aristotelian four causes: 1) matter and what accompanies it; 2) the definition and its parts (corresponding to the form); 3) the agent and what goes with it; and finally 4) the purpose and what goes with it. By what accompanies these causes or goes with it, obviously al-Fārābi meant any factors that go with the cause in question, such as the agent and his tools, the goal sought and the means of attaining it. Each one of these causes, he then goes on to say, is either proximate or ultimate, essential or accidental, more general or more particular, and potential or actual. Each one of these causes may be taken as the middle term of a given syllogism.

Now, the objects of demonstration are either universal or particular; therefore, the premises of universal demonstrations must be universal. Such premises include particulars, and although al-Fārābi does not mention it, particular premises do not yield any conclusions. In addition, for the conclusions of such demonstrations to be necessary, they must rest on necessary premises. Al-Fārābi then distinguishes between categorical and conditional premises. Necessary categorical premises are those whose predicates are necessarily related to their subject; whereas conditional premises are those whose corollaries are necessary. However, every

5. Cf. *Kitāb al-Burhān*, p. 26.

conditional proposition can be converted to a categorical one. For instance, the statement 'If the two sides of a triangle A are equal to the two sides of a triangle B, and the angles enclosed between their parallel sides are equal, those two triangles would be equal.'[6] (This conditional proposition can be converted to a categorical proposition, as follows: Every two triangles, such as A and B, whose sides are equal and in which the angles enclosed between their parallel sides are equal, are equal.)

The relation between cause and demonstration is further characterized as follows. Demonstrations that yield the knowledge of the cause presuppose the knowledge of the existence of the object, either by demonstrations known as proofs (*dalā'il*) or by recourse to experience. Once we know the existence of the object, we can then proceed to seek its causes.

Each of the four causes, al-Fārābi then argues, may form the answer to the question 'Why?', once we have ascertained the existence of the object or its corollary. Thus, we are justified in asking 'Why do humans die?', once we have learnt that in fact they die. Then, we can answer, 'Because they are made up of contraries (*material* cause); or because they are living, dying rational beings (*formal*); or because it is better for them to die (the *final* cause); or because their agent or preserver is changeable (*efficient* cause).'[7]

Some causes are not easy to ascertain at first glance, nor easily explained to be the causes of given effects. For example, if we ask 'Why does the vine shed its leaves in winter?', we may answer, 'Because its leaves are broad', which is an essential cause. However, it is not clear from that statement how this is the cause of the vine shedding its leaves in winter, unless it is supplemented by reference to proximate causes. Thus, we would then have to say 'Because humidity, which causes the leaves to hold together, causes broader leaves to be shed faster.'

The same thing, we are then told, may have numerous causes, while a multitude of things could have a single cause, in point of genus, species or proportion. For instance, the echo and the rainbow have one cause generically; namely, the reflection of sound or light; whereas the rainbow and a reflection in the mirror have one cause specifically; namely, the

6. Ibid., p. 27.
7. Ibid., p. 42.

refraction (*in'ikās*) of light, owing to cloud in the first case and glass in the second case.[8]

Things whose cause are one may be causes of each other, the farthest cause being the cause of them all. For example, if we ask, 'Why does the water of the Nile abound in winter; and why is the air at the end of the month similar to the air in winter?', the cause in both of these cases is found to be the declension of the light of the moon. Al-Fārābi then lists the causal sequence in which all the above phenomena stand with respect to each other. Thus, the cause of the abundance of the water of the Nile is the abundance of humidity in the air, whose cause is the similarity of air at that time to that of air in winter, whose cause is the low heat in the air, owing to moonlight, whose cause is the recession of the light of the moon, facing the earth, owing to its proximity to the sun. Therefore, we may conclude that the proximity of the moon to the sun is, in fact, the cause of all these phenomena, each of which is the cause of the other.[9]

The various senses of the term, 'intellect' ('aql)

The problem of the intellect or reason, expressed in Arabic in one word – *'aql* – was at the center of philosophical speculation from the earliest times. Aristotle raised the many questions that arise in connection with this highest faculty of the soul, but left many aspects of these questions unanswered. Alexander of Aphrodisias (*c.* 205), one of his earlier commentators, dealt with this question in his treatise *On the Intellect*, which found its way into Arabic and was often referred to by the Arab philosophers. Of the latter, al-Kindi (d. *c.* 866) wrote the first treatise on the intellect, which set the tone for future discussions of the nature of the intellect and its fourfold divisions, as given by al-Kindi.

In his own treatise, *On the Meanings of the Intellect* (*Fī Ma'āni al-'Aql*), al-Fārābi begins by giving a list of the meanings of the intellect or reason, as used by the general public, the Mutakallimun, and Aristotle in *Analytica Posteriora*, the *Nicomachean Ethics*, the *De Anima*[10] and the *Metaphysics*.

8. Ibid., p. 43. The text says 'a glossy iron', from which mirrors were made in al-Fārābi's day.
9. Ibid., p. 44.
10. *De anima, III*, 429 *a* 10f.

1. With respect to the meaning of 'reason' as used by the public, when they describe a person as reasonable (*'āqil*), it clearly refers to prudence (*ta'aqqul*) or sound judgment in the determination of what is right, as against the determination of what is wrong, generally referred to as cunning or perfidy. This meaning, al-Fārābi then adds, corresponds to what Aristotle means by prudence or the faculty of determining what is right or wrong indifferently. Some people, al-Fārābi observes, have questioned this meaning, stipulating that, to be prudent, a person must partake of some religion (*dīn*), and that a wicked person, however resourceful, should not be described as prudent.[11]
2. As for the sense in which the Mutakallimun use the term 'reason', referring to certain actions enjoined by reason or repudiated by reason, they simply mean by 'reason' in this context what is generally received by the public as a whole or for the most part.
3. The reason mentioned by Aristotle in *Analytica Posteriora* (*Kitāb al-Burhān*) refers to a 'faculty of the soul whereby man is able to attain certainty by recourse to universal, true and necessary premises, known neither by deduction [*qiyās*] nor reflection, but rather naturally and instinctively'.[12] This faculty is that part of the soul by which knowledge is gained, directly and intuitively, of the premises that are the first principles of the theoretical sciences.
4. The other meaning of 'reason' mentioned in the sixth book of the *Nicomachean Ethics* refers to that part of the soul which is able to gain, through habituation and prolonged experience, a certain apprehension of premises pertaining to volitional matters, which are susceptible of being sought or shunned. This is a form of prudence whereby one is able to apprehend the principles of practical or voluntary matters, in the same way as the principles of the theoretical sciences are apprehended. This reason, mentioned in the sixth book of the *Nicomachean Ethics*, grows with age, so that only people who are old and experienced can excel in using it and are rightly called people of sound judgment.

11. *Maqālah fī Ma'āni al-'Aql* (Dieterici), p. 40.
12. Ibid., p. 40. Cf. Aristotle, *Analytica Posteriora*, II, Chapters 19–20.

Aristotle, it may be recalled, distinguishes six modes of knowledge in the *Nicomachean Ethics, VI*: scientific knowledge (*episteme*), practical wisdom (*phronesis*), philosophical wisdom (*sophia*), intuitive reason (*noūs*) and art (*techne*). He describes practical wisdom, which corresponds to the above virtue which al-Fārābi designates as prudence (*ta'aqqul*), as the mark of the man 'who is able to deliberate well about what is good and expedient for himself, not in some particular respect, but about what sorts of things conduce to the good life in general'.[13]

5. Next, al-Fārābi refers to that reason which Aristotle mentions in *De Anima* and divides, as al-Fārābi puts it, into potential, actual, acquired and active reason. The first is a part or faculty of the soul, al-Fārābi goes on to say, disposed to receive the essences or forms of all entities, as divested of their matter. The forms so received are called intelligibles, in reference to the intellect or that part of the soul which abstracts them from matter. This part may be said to be analogous to matter in the same sense in which a piece of wax is said to be analogous to the imprint made on it. It is that faculty of the soul which Aristotle has called potential reason, and is susceptible of becoming identified with its object, just as the piece of wax and its imprint are identified. However, prior to the reception of the forms of existing entities which this faculty abstracts from matter, such a faculty of the soul is purely potential. However, once the forms of existing entities are received by that faculty, it becomes reason in act, or actual reason, by virtue of the actual intelligibles inhering in it. However, in that respect, actual reason and the actual intelligibles are one and the same. However, despite this identification, we are told by al-Fārābi, the actual intelligibles are entirely distinguishable from the original forms inherent in matter, since in that capacity the forms are determined according to time, position, quality, quantity and other physical properties. Once they become actual intelligibles, they become free of all these conditions and may in that sense be described as pure intelligibles.

Such intelligibles become, once actualized, parts of the sum-total of existing entities in the world. Even intelligibles that were never embedded

13. *Nicomachean Ethics, VI*, 1140 *a* 25f.

in matter become, upon being apprehended by the actual intellect, parts of the world of existing entities. In apprehending such immaterial entities, actual reason, which has now reached the level of acquired reason (*'aql muktasab*), does not need to abstract them from their matter, in exactly the same way it apprehends itself as an actual intellect. In that act of direct apprehension, the acquired intellect is analogous to the subject of the actual intelligible, in its relation to the actual intellect preceding it, being analogous to the relation of form to matter. The faculty of the soul we called the potential intellect is analogous at that point to matter.

Once the level of the acquired intellect, which may be described as the zenith of the human process of cognition, is attained, the process of ascent from the potential to the actual, and finally the acquired, intellect is reversed and the downward process of descent begins. Thus, we would have the following descending scheme. The immaterial intelligibles (represented as somewhat analogous to Plato's Ideas) are followed by the acquired intellect, then actual reason, followed by the potential reason, followed by the natural order with the compound and simple bodies (i.e. the four elements) that make it up. In that scheme, the acquired intellect marks the borderline between the material and intelligible worlds, at the lowest level of which stands the Active Intellect, which marks in the Neoplatonic cosmology of al-Fārābi the tenth emanation from the First Being and the mover of the sublunary world, as we will see in the next chapter.

The Active Intellect

At this point, al-Fārābi proceeds to describe this Active Intellect, which Aristotle mentions briefly in *De Anima, III.* This Active Intellect, according to al-Fārābi, is 'an immaterial form which is not in matter and could not subsist in matter at all. It is in a sense an actual reason analogous to the acquired intellect.'[14]

This Active Intellect, he goes on to state, is the agency that causes the potential intellect, as well as the potential intelligibles, to become actual; its relation to the potential intellect being similar to that of the sun to the

14. *Fī Ma'āni al-'Aql*, p. 46.

eye. He pursues the analogy of the sun and the eye in some detail, and argues that just as the eye is potentially incapable of vision, so long as darkness persists, and will only become actually seeing once the light of the sun dissipates the darkness, so is the Active Intellect in relation to the potential intellect, to which it imparts that power of apprehension analogous to the light of the sun.[15]

However, despite this exalted role ascribed to the Active Intellect, at both the intellectual and cosmological levels, al-Fārābi regards it as subordinate to the First Principle, from which the intellectual world directly and the material world indirectly emanate. The reason he gives is that the action of this supermundane principle is neither continuous nor constant, not owing to any passivity proper to it, but rather its dependence on the passive matter on which it must act. Sometimes that matter is wanting or is not sufficiently disposed to receive the forms emanating from the First Principle, owing to some impediment or other, and thus its action is interrupted. Hence, two things are necessary to ensure that the action of the Active Intellect is possible: a material substratum and the absence of any impediments, neither of which is within its power. This goes to show, argues al-Fārābi, that the Active Intellect is far from being identified with the First Principle of all things. This First Principle is identified, by al-Fārābi, with the One or God, upon whom both the Active Intellect and the material substrata on which it acts depend.[16] Even the heavenly bodies are then shown to depend on that First Principle, both for their being and the motion they derive from the first heaven, which depends in turn on the Unmoved Mover, as Aristotle argues in *Metaphysics, XII*.[17]

To assess al-Fārābi's theory of the intellect, in both its epistemological and its cosmological aspects, which he develops chiefly in light of what Aristotle states in *De Anima*, the *Nicomachean Ethics* and the *Metaphysics*, some comments are in order. Aristotle, it will be recalled, was far more reticent on the knotty question of the Active Intellect than al-Fārābi is willing to admit. In *De Anima, III*, Aristotle clearly distinguishes between potential and actual reason (*noūs*) and asserts that, in the act of thought,

15. Ibid., p. 47.
16. Cf. *Risālah fi'l-'Aql*, pp. 33f.
17. *Metaphysics, XII*, 1072 *a* 22.

the mind and its object become one and the same.[18] He then goes on to distinguish in the soul between 1) the matter 'which is potentially all the particulars included in that class, and [2)] the cause which is productive in the sense that it makes them all'.[19] The first is then described as that which *becomes* all things; whereas the second is described as that which *makes* all things, and is compared to light which makes potential colors into actual colors. Apart from this distinction, Aristotle does not shed much light on the relation of those two parts of the soul, the potential and the actual; this gave rise, both in antiquity and in the Middle Ages, to endless controversies. Some, like Alexander of Aphrodisias, identified the Active Intellect with God; others, like St. Thomas Aquinas (d. 1274), with a power within the soul. Still others, like al-Fārābi, as we have seen, and Ibn Sina a generation later, identified it with that supermundane agency which lies on the periphery of the world of generation and corruption.

For the reader of Aristotle, nothing could be farther from his apparent intent. 'Mind in this sense', as he says in *De Anima, III*, 429 *a* 18, 'is separable [*choristos*], impassible [*apathis*] and unmixed [*amigis*]'; he then adds that this mind alone is immortal and eternal. However, Aristotle has nowhere assigned to this mind, called active (*poetikos*) by Alexander, the kind of cosmological function that al-Fārābi and Ibn Sina have, in Neoplatonic fashion, assigned to it, as both the mover of the sublunary world and the 'giver of forms' (*Wāhib al-Ṣuwar*), from which the substantive forms of immaterial entities, as Ibn Sina puts it, emanate.

For Aristotle, the Active Intellect appears, then, to be a purely universal and immaterial principle of intellection, which is the counterpart or antipode of the material universe and, like it, is eternal and everlasting. Like Aristotle, al-Fārābi recognized that the Active Intellect is clearly distinguishable from the First Principle or Unmoved Mover, on which it actually depends. But unlike Aristotle, he describes it as an emanation, ten times removed, from the First Principle, or the One of Plotinus. Even here, al-Fārābi goes well beyond Plotinus, for whom the ultimate principle of motion is the second emanation from the One or the

18. *De anima, III*, 429 *a* 20f. and 430 *a* 2.
19. Ibid., III, 430 *a* 10f.

Universal Soul (*Psyche*), which may be described as the mediator between the intelligible and the material worlds. Without this mediator, so to speak, the First Intellect (or *Noūs*) cannot possibly act on that lower world. It was, perhaps, out of his desire to bridge the tremendous gap between the intelligible and the material worlds that al-Fārābi felt compelled to introduce that series of ten intellects, of which the Active Intellect is the last. He did not accord in the process to the Universal Soul its rightful role as the link between the two worlds and, as just mentioned, as the principle of motion or generation in the lower world.

6

Emanation versus Creation

The Neoplatonic legacy

One of the earliest philosophical works to be translated into Arabic, probably from Syriac, was a treatise known in Arabic as *Uthulugia Arisṭuṭālīs* (*The Theology of Aristotle*) or *Kitāb al-Rubūbiyah* (*Book of Divinity*). Its translator was a certain 'Abd al-Masīh Ibn Nā'imah al-Ḥim'i (d. 835), and it is known today to be a paraphrase of the last three *Enneads* of Plotinus; or *Enneads*, IV, V and VI, probably by Plotinus's own disciple and biographer Porphyry of Tyre, author of the famous *Isagoge*, or introduction to the *Categories* of Aristotle.

This *Uthulugia* had a very wide circulation in philosophical circles and was commented on by al-Kindi, Ibn Sina and others. It is quoted extensively in al-Fārābi's *Reconciliation of Plato and Aristotle*, already discussed.

A similar Neoplatonic treatise, known in Arabic as *al-Khayr al-Mahḍ* (*The Pure Good*), consisted of thirty-two out of the 289 propositions of the *Elements of Theology*, by the late Athenian Neoplatonist, Proclus (d. 485). This treatise was translated into Arabic by an unknown translator around the beginning of the tenth century and was later translated into Latin and circulated in philosophical circles in the thirteenth century as the *Liber de Causis*.

Those two treatises embodied the Neoplatonic worldview, which al-Fārābi was the first to develop in the Arab-Muslim world. The pivotal point of that worldview was the theory of emanation (*fayḍ*, *ṣudūr*), which Plotinus had introduced as a means of bridging the gap between the intelligible and the material worlds, on the one hand, and giving a coherent account of the coming-to-be of the universe from the One (*to Hen*) or First Principle, through a process of gradual overflowing or diffusion, on the other. This process generally known as emanation gives rise to the intellect (*noūs*), the soul (*psyche*) and the world of nature, in succession.

The chief merit of that theory is that it appeared to give a rationally credible account of the coming-to-be of the universe from the One throughout eternity. It dispensed thereby with the two presuppositions of the rival creationist theory, according to which the world was created by God out of nothing and in time by an act of divine fiat (*amr*), as the Qur'an expresses in a number of verses.[1]

In addition, the theory of emanation accorded reason an exalted position in the hierarchy of being and set up the soul as the link between the intelligible and material worlds. So long as it is incarcerated in the body, this soul will yearn for return to its original abode in the higher world and will eventually be liberated through the therapeutic study of philosophy.

The creationist thesis, explicitly and eloquently laid down in the Qur'an, was never in vogue in Muslim philosophical circles, because it implied that the world was created peremptorily and miraculously by God, whose decrees cannot by questioned. He creates the world out of nothing at a time of His own choosing, a thesis that, for the philosophers, ran counter to the proposition that God cannot be supposed to act capriciously, without any regard to the laws of reason. Some philosophers, such as Ibn Rushd (Averroes) (d. 1198) went so far as to question the claims of the Mutakallimun that the Qur'an itself asserts unambiguously that God has created the world out of nothing and in time. For those verses which refer to God as 'He who created the heavens and the earth in six days

1. See e.g. Qur'an 2:47 and 2:117.

while His Throne was upon water' (Qur'an 11:7) or that He created the world and 'then arose to heaven, which consisted of smoke' (Qur'an 41:11), Averroes argues in his *Decisive Treatise* (*Fasl al-Maqūl*), imply on the face of it that the creation of the world was preceded by the Throne, the water, the smoke and the time that measures their duration.[2] In addition, creation in time clashed with Aristotle's view that creation in time entails logically that there was a time when time was not; in other words, that before the beginning of time, time already existed. It also implies, as Aristotle also argued, that substances, being the most primary of existing entities, cannot be supposed to be destructible. For, were they destructible, everything else would be destructible, including time, and if time, then motion, of which time is the measure, and this has been shown to be absurd.[3]

It is to be noted that Plato, who allowed for the creation of the world in time by the Demiurge, or the Father of All, could not reconcile himself to the concept of creation *ex nihilo*, and held instead that the universe was created out of a formless matter, which he calls the foster-mother of becoming, or simply the receptacle.[4]

The nature of the First Being or the One

Before engaging in the discussion of emanation, al-Fārābi opens the *Virtuous City* (*al-Madinah al-Fāḍilah*) by asserting that the First Being (*al-Awwal*) is the cause of all existing entities. He then proceeds to characterize this Being as one 'whose existence is the best and most ancient [*aqdan*] existence, nothing better or more ancient than which could exist'.[5] As such, the First Being is entirely free from the imperfection of potentiality or possibility and is not susceptible of any privation (*'adam*). Therefore, it is everlasting and is entirely self-sufficient. In addition, the First Being, al-Fārābi asserts, is entirely uncaused, free of matter and without form, 'since form can only exist in matter',[6] and its being has no purpose or end external to itself.

2. Cf. *Fasl al-Maqūl*, p. 41.
3. Cf. *Metaphysics, XII*, 1071 *b* 5f.
4. Cf. *Timaeus*, 49 *b*.
5. Cf. *Al-Madīnah al-Fāḍilah*, p. 23.
6. Ibid., p. 24.

In deference to official Islamic doctrine, al-Fārābi goes on to state that the First Being has no partner (*sharīk*) who shares in its being or perfection, for if it did, this partner would be made up of that which is peculiar to it and that which it shares with the First, and thus would be composite and accordingly radically different from the First, whose essence is simple and indivisible.[7]

Nor can the First have an opposite, or else the two would nullify each other. For, it is of the essence of two opposites that the one is where the other is not, or is not where the other is and, as such, is corruptible. However, were the First corruptible, its subsistence or duration would not be part of its essence and, accordingly, would depend for its existence on something else. As such, it would cease to be the First or Everlasting Being.

Moreover, by virtue of its indivisibility, the First does not admit of definition (*ḥadd*). For, the statement that explains its meaning, or definitional formula, would denote the two parts which constitute its essence, and these would be equivalent to the causes of its existence, as is the case with the parts of every composite, or the matter and form that make up material compounds.

Contrasted with other existing entities, the essence of the First is that whereby it is distinct from all other things, and this is precisely that whereby it is one. For one of the meanings of unity is that specific property whereby it is distinguishable from everything else. In that sense, the First is not only one, but is more worthy of the attribute of unity than anything else.[8]

Having established that the First neither is matter nor has any material substratum, al-Fārābi concludes that it must be an intellect in act (*'aql bi'l-fi'l*). For what impedes matter from being an intellect or apprehending in act is the matter in which an entity subsists. Thus, whatever does not require matter for it to exist is essentially an intellect in act. By the same token, the First is an intelligible (*ma'qūl*) in act, since matter is precisely that which impedes an entity from becoming an intelligible in act. More specifically, al-Farābi then adds, the First is intelligible precisely insofar as

7. Ibid., p. 25.
8. Ibid., p. 30.

it is an intellect, since it does not require any external agency to cause it to become the object of its own intellection. In short, the First is at one and the same time the act, subject and object of its own intellection; or, as Aristotle puts it in *Metaphysics*, *XII*, 1074 *b* 34, thought thinking thought (*Nous, noesis, noeseos, 'aql, wa 'āqil wa ma'qūl*). Humankind, by contrast, al-Fārābi explains, is radically different. For the object of thought for humankind is not an intelligible in act, but rather an intelligible in potentiality, or a potential intelligible. Nor is humankind the agent and the act of thought at one and the same time, as was the case with the First.[9]

It is to be noted at this point that in identifying the First with intellect or thought, al-Fārābi was unwittingly breaking with the Neoplatonic tradition, as represented primarily by its founder, Plotinus, for whom the One is entirely transcendent, lying above being and thought. Out of its superabundant goodness, Plotinus argues, the One gives rise by way of emanation to the first genuine being, the intellect or *noūs*, which Plotinus sometimes calls the 'second good'. With *noūs*, it might then be said, being and thought emerge into the broad daylight of reality, beyond which the One lies in a mysterious and indeterminate way. Aristotle, at the philosophical level, and the Qur'an, at the religious level, removed that indeterminateness. The former regarded God or the First Principle as an immovable and eternal substance (*ousia*) or actuality (*Metaphysics*, XII, 1072 *a* 25); whereas the latter has distinguished God as the 'only One ... the Everlasting [*samad*] ... None is His equal' (Qur'an 112). For both Aristotle and the Qur'an, God is in the fullest sense the Supreme Being and the supreme object of thought. For Plotinus, as already mentioned, the One is above and beyond both being and thought.

The other attributes of God or the First, as given by al-Fārābi, have a distinct Qur'anic ring. He is *'alim* (knowing), *ḥakīm* (wise), *ḥaqq* (true) and *ḥayy* (living). He is knowing, al-Fārābi explains, in the sense that, in knowing everything including Himself, He does not require the assistance of anything or anybody other than Himself; wise in the sense that His knowledge is the highest and most enduring. He is true insofar as truth is

9. Ibid., p. 31.

equivalent to existence, of which He has the highest share. Another meaning of 'truth' is the correspondence of knowledge with being, which is a characteristic of the First, who knows Himself as He really is. Finally, He is living in the sense that the living is the 'one who knows the best object of thought [*ma'qūl*] in the best manner of thought ['*aql*]', which, as we have seen, is equivalent to Himself. Another meaning of 'living' refers to any entity that has attained its highest perfection, of which, as the Perfect Being, the First is most deserving.[10]

Such a being, al-Fārābi goes on to argue, must be regarded as supremely beautiful and, as such, as supremely happy. For he partakes of a pleasure that we cannot understand or fathom, the object of which is himself, as the most beautiful and glamorous of objects. Now, since pleasure is the natural accompaniment of love (*'ishq*), it follows that the First also partakes of love, both as subject and object (*'āshiq wa ma'shūq*).[11]

The intellect, as the first emanation

The First, then, is that Being, al-Fārābi goes on to argue, from whom must arise by a 'necessity of nature', as the Scholastic theologians tended to call it, 'all those existing entities which do not derive their existence from human will or choice',[12] through a process of overflowing or emanation, which adds nothing to the perfection of the First, who is their source, but simply as an act of supererogatory generosity or bounty on its part, as Proclus expressed it. Finally, al-Fārābi asserts, the act of overflowing, being entirely necessary, cannot be deterred by any impediment, either from the First or from anything external to it.

The first emanation from the First, designated by al-Fārābi as the second being, is an incorporeal and immaterial entity, or intellect, which apprehends itself and apprehends the First. Insofar as it apprehends the First, it gives rise to the second intellect, or third being in this hierarchical scale; while in apprehending itself it gives rise to the first heaven. The third being, likewise, apprehends itself as well as the First. In apprehending itself, it gives rise to

10. Ibid., p. 32.
11. Ibid., p. 37. Cf. *al-Siyāsah al-Madaniyah*, p. 47.
12. Ibid., p. 38.

the firmament of the fixed stars; while in apprehending the First, it gives rise to the third intellect, followed by the fourth, the fifth, the sixth, the seventh, the eighth and the ninth intellects, with the corresponding spheres of Jupiter, Mars, the sun, Venus and Mercury, respectively. The series of intellects, however, closes with the tenth, which, in apprehending itself, gives rise to the sphere of the moon. This is that supermundane agency which dominates the world of generation and corruption,[13] and is the supreme object of human cognition, descibed by al-Fārābi as conjunction (*ittisāl*), as the theory of knowledge, discused earlier, has shown.

The heavenly bodies

The tenth intellect marks in a sense the point of demarcation between the intelligible and material worlds, by virtue of its function as the supermundane agency that governs the material world. Al-Fārābi dwells on the properties of the heavenly bodies, which begin with the first heaven and terminate with the moon. He describes the first heaven as one in genus, but many in species, although each species thereof consists of one specific body, which cannot share any of its properties with any other body. However, al-Fārābi admits that the heavenly bodies share with material entities the property that they have their own substrata (*mawdū'āt*),[14] which are analogous to matter as well as their own forms. These forms, however, have no contraries and their substrata are not susceptible of receiving any other forms or any contrariety. That is why these substrata, being of a special kind, do not bar those bodies from belonging to the category of intellects. For, by virtue of its form, each heavenly body is able to apprehend the intellect corresponding to it, as well as the First itself.

However, al-Fārābi observes, because of their association with their substrata, the heavenly bodies do not belong to the category of pure intellects. Nevertheless, like the pure intellects, they are capable of partaking of pleasures, self-love and self-adoration of which their immaterial causes, whether the pure intellects or the First, actually

13. Ibid., pp. 44f. Cf. *al-Siyāsah al-Madaniyah*, pp. 52f.
14. The substrata in question refer to ether, or the fifth element.

partake, but to a far lesser degree. Moreover, they are blessed with the noblest of shapes, which is the spherical, and the noblest of properties, which is the emission of light.[15]

Al-Fārābi, in investing the heavenly bodies with divine properties, was actually continuing an old tradition going back to the Babylonians, according to which the heavenly bodies were worshiped as gods. An echo of this tradition is to be found in the Qur'an itself, which refers to the worship of the stars by the ancestors of Abraham, against which the Father of the Semites is said to have rebelled.[16] Even Aristotle refers, with a certain measure of approval, to the recognition of the divinity of the stars by the ancients, both Greeks and barbarians (or non-Greeks). In *Metaphysics*, XII, 1074 *b* 1, he regards it as an 'inspired utterance' that 'our forefathers in the most remote ages, have handed down to their posterity a tradition in the form of a myth that these (heavenly) bodies are gods'.[17]

Al-Kindi, the first Muslim philosopher, is even more emphatic in attributing intelligence to the heavenly bodies. First, as the proximate causes of our being rational 'in accordance with God's decree', he argues, the heavenly bodies must be regarded as the causes of our being rational. For were they lacking in intelligence, it would be impossible for them to be the causes of our being rational. Secondly, of the three faculties of the soul – the rational, the passionate and the appetitive – the rational is the highest, since it contributes to the perfection of the entities who possess it, rather than their mere survival. The heavenly bodies, being indestructible, must possess this faculty to the exclusion of the other two. Thirdly, if we compare the circumference of the earth with that of the universe at large, al-Kindi argues, and then compare the bulk of humankind with the bulk of the earth and the other creatures inhabiting it, we will find how infinitesimal is the proportion of humankind to the universe at large. Thus, if humankind were the only rational species in the universe at large, the proportion of rational creatures to the rest of creation would be infinitesimal and this would detract from the perfection of God and His

15. Ibid., p. 54.
16. Qur'an 21:52, 6:78.
17. Cf. also *Heavens*, *I*, 270 *a* 15.

wisdom, since undoubtedly the rational creature is superior to the irrational. Therefore, God in His immense wisdom, al-Kindi concludes, has 'decreed that those creatures which are not subject to corruption, throughout the appointed term of their existence [i.e. the heavenly bodies] will far surpass those which are subject to it',[18] and therefore will possess the higher faculty of intelligence or reason.

The material world

Beneath the heavenly bodies in the scale of emanation comes the material world, made up of those entities which have not attained their perfection initially, but are susceptible of attaining it in stages. They include natural and voluntary entities or their derivatives.

Natural entities include in the first instance the four elements of fire, air, water and earth, or the like, such as vapor and flame. These are followed by minerals, such as stones, and their derivatives, which include plants and animals, whether rational or irrational. The chief characteristic of these material compounds is that they are made up of matter and form in such a way that neither can exist independently of the other. What distinguishes one from the other is the fact that form is the principle of actuality or perfection, and matter is the principle of potentiality in the compound.[19]

How compounds arise from their constitutive, simple elements is described by al-Fārābi as a form of admixture or combination (*ikhtilāt*). First, the elements combine with each other to generate numerous contrary bodies; then these bodies combine with the elements to generate numerous bodies of contrary forms. It is characteristic of such bodies that they possess certain active and passive faculties, whereby they act on each other or are affected by each other, on the one hand, and certain motive faculties whereby they are able to move spontaneously. Then, those bodies interact with the four elements and with each other, in the way mentioned above, but are acted upon by the heavenly bodies. This gives rise in due course to a great variety of admixtures or combinations, generating a great variety of entities – mineral, vegetative, animal and human.

18. *Rasā'il al-Kindi, I,* p. 256. Cf. M. Fakhry, *A History of Islamic Philosophy*, pp. 82f.
19. *Al-Madīnah al-Fāḍilah*, p. 47.

How the heavenly bodies contribute to the generation of material entities is explained in terms of a certain community of nature. For the nature of the heavenly bodies, which generates their circular motion, gives rise to prime matter, common to all lower bodies in the material world. Those bodies are made up of matter and form, and are subject to the reception, in succession, of contrary qualities, by virtue of their common (prime) matter. That explains, according to al-Fārābi, why the individual cannot last forever, but only the species. For it is a law of nature that every such individual be succeeded by its like either at once or after a certain interval. All this takes place under the influence of the heavenly bodies, which either assist or oppose the emergence of such individuals. This process, however, is not haphazard, according to al-Fārābi, but is subject to a law of merit (*isti'hāl*) proper to the matter and to another law proper to the form. Justice, he adds, consists in the fact that merit is fulfilled at one time or another in alternation.[20]

The human soul and its faculties

When we cross the line of demarcation between the intelligible and the terrestrial worlds, the downward process of emanation is reversed and the process of generation becomes one of ascent from the lowest to the highest. Thus, from prime matter, as we have seen, the elements and their material compounds, consisting of minerals, plants, animals and humans, arise. Accordingly, al-Fārābi proceeds to discuss the human soul and its faculties, which begin with the nutritive, followed by the sensitive, the desiderative, the imaginative and finally the rational, with its two subdivisions, the theoretical and the practical.[21]

Each of these faculties has its own auxiliaries, residing in the lower organs of the body, such as the liver, the spleen, the kidney and the gall-bladder, which are all subservient to the principal organ, the heart.

The auxiliary organs of the sensitive faculty are the five senses residing in the eyes, the ears and the rest of the five sense-organs, which all subserve the heart also. The imaginative faculty, on the other hand, has no

20. Ibid., p. 67.
21. Ibid., p. 70.

auxiliaries other than the sense-organs that it governs, and like them is located in the heart.

The same is true of the rational faculty, which presides over the lower faculties of imagination, sensation and nutrition, and has no auxiliaries. It also resides in the heart.

The desiderative faculty (*nuzū'iyah*) is then defined as the faculty whereby one desires or shuns what is an object of either thought or action, giving rise to will. This is the faculty of desiring what has already been apprehended through sense, imagination or reason as something to be acquired or relinquished.

Bodily actions are performed by bodily organs that subserve the desiderative faculty. They consist of nerves and muscles spread throughout these organs, such as hands and feet, which are the instruments or tools of the desiderative faculty. Action, in general, is consequent on the knowledge of the object, through the rational, the imaginative or the sensitive faculties.[22] Al-Fārābi then dwells on the interrelation of the bodily organs, of which, as we have seen, the chief is the heart, followed by the brain. The heart, he explains, is the source of natural heat, which is the principle of life in animals, moderated by the brain. The reason he gives is that the action of the imaginative and rational faculties is possible only when the heat of the heart is of a definite degree, neither in excess nor in defect. The same is true of the subsidiary faculties of memory or recollection.

The reproductive faculty is later in appearance and has two seats, the heart and the reproductive organs. These organs are twofold: one that prepares the matter to receive the form of the animal, and is identified with the female sex-organ; the second which prepares the form of the animal and resides in the male sex-organ. The organ that subserves the heart in providing the matter of the animal is the womb, whereas the organ that provides the form of humans or other animals is the male organ that provides semen. This semen is similar to rennet, which causes milk to curdle and turn into sour milk. It is generated by the muscles that lie under the pubic hair, assisted by the two testicles.[23]

22. Ibid., p. 73.
23. Ibid., p. 79.

When the blood receives from the semen the power that moves or actualizes the human form, the heart is formed. If, together with the nutritive faculty, the power that disposes *matter* arises, then the rest of the organs of the body will take the shape of a female. If, on the other hand, the nutritive faculty is accompanied by the power that gives rise to the *form*, then the rest of the organs will take the shape of a male. Then, female and male organs follow the corresponding power. It is characteristic of the male organs, al-Fārābi explains, to generate greater heat, associated with the psychological emotions of anger and cruelty, unlike the weaker female organs, which are associated with such emotions as compassion and mercy.[24]

The rational faculty is defined by al-Fārābi as 'a certain trait [*hay'ah*] inhering in a matter which is disposed to receive the images [*rusūm*] of intelligibles, and is thus potentially a material intellect as well as a potential intelligible'.[25] The principal subdivisions of the intellect are then given as: potential or material (*hayūlāni*), habitual (*bi'l-malakah, in habitu*) and acquired (*mustafād*).[26] For the potential intellect to be actualized, an immaterial agency that is an intellect in act must impart to it something analogous to the light of the sun, which makes the potentially visible actually visible, and the potentially colored actually colored. This agency is the Active Intellect, which is the tenth in the series of emanations from the One.[27] This intellect, discussed at length in Chapter 5, is described in a short tract, entitled the *Principal Questions* (*'Uyūn al-Masā'il*), as 'immaterial, and will survive the death of the body and is not susceptible of any corruption. It is a unique substance and is man himself in truth.'[28]

Prophecy and the imaginative faculty

Although al-Fārābi refers in his tabulation of the faculties (or parts) of the soul to the principal Aristotelian list of nutritive, sensitive, desiderative, imaginative and rational faculties, as we have seen, he has accorded the

24. Ibid., pp. 80f.
25. Ibid., p. 82.
26. Cf. *'Uyūn al-Masā'il* (Dieterici), p. 64.
27. Cf. *al-Madinah*, p. 84.
28. Cf. *'Uyūn al-Masā'il* (Dieterici), p. 64.

rational and imaginative faculties a special place in his psychology and epistemology. Having already discussed his theory of the intellect in some detail, we should now turn to the role he attaches to the imaginative faculty in dreaming, prophesying and the representation of intelligible forms.

The imaginative faculty, according to al-Fārābi, is intermediate between the sensitive and the rational. Its chief function is to retain sense-images and combine or separate them at will. However, it has another function, which consists in simulating (*muhākāt*) the sensible forms stored in it and, in some cases, the rational and desiderative forms, as well as the bodily humors. As an instance, he cites the way in which the imaginative faculty is able to simulate bodily humidity by imparting sensations of humidity experienced in swimming, or bodily dryness, heat or cold by imparting corresponding sensations of dryness, heat and cold.[29]

As for rational forms, they are not received by the imaginative faculty as they are in themselves, but rather as sensible representations, simulating them. Similarly, in the case of the desiderative faculty, the actions of the imaginative faculty are ones of simulation. Thus, if the imaginative faculty finds that faculty disposed to a certain sensation or emotion, such as anger or lust, it proceeds at once to mobilize the subsidiary organs that subserve those emotions, to move in the direction of the emotion in question. Thus, if the bodily humor inclines towards sexual desire or lust, the imaginative faculty simulates that humor proper to the sexual act, and accordingly the sexual organs are stimulated, not by an actual desire or object at that time, but rather by an imaginary desire or object. Sometimes, a person will wake up, hit another or run away without any outside cause, but a purely imaginary one.

Moreover, the imaginative faculty, being associated with the rational faculty, in both its theoretical and practical capacities, is sometimes able to represent certain particulars in dreams or 'veridical revelation' (*nu'ya sādiqah*), by virtue of the light it receives from the Active Intellect. These representations are possible both in sleep and in waking, although in sleep they tend to be more frequent.[30]

29. Ibid., p. 88.
30. Ibid., p. 92.

In fact, the imaginative faculty may attain in some people a superlative pitch and, in such cases, is not fully dominated by the sensations received from outside. Instead, it is liberated during the waking state from these sensations, just as happens during sleep; and then the forms of absent sensations are represented under the influence of the Active Intellect, as though they were perfectly real. When those representations reach the pitch of beauty and perfection, the visionary, or inspired person, will proclaim the majesty and splendor of God and will perceive strange objects, the likes of which are not found in the real world. It may even happen that such individuals, whose imaginative faculty has reached its highest pitch, will be able to receive from the Active Intellect visions of present or future occurrences, or of their sensible similitudes. They may also receive the similitudes of immaterial intelligibles, as well as the rest of the higher entities, and perceive them visually. Then, they will have achieved, by virtue of the intelligibles they have received, the power of prophesying divine things. 'This is the highest rank which the imaginative faculty can attain and the highest rank man may achieve by virtue of his imaginative faculty.'[31]

Below this rank, al-Fārābi goes on to argue, is that of those who perceive all these things, either in their sleep or waking state, and are able to imagine them in themselves, but do not perceive them visually. Below this rank still is that of those who perceive those things in their sleep only and express their perceptions in terms of analogies, symbols, enigmas or simulations.

This class of visionaries is divided into those who perceive particulars but not intelligibles, and those who perceive intelligibles but not particulars, in their waking state, on the one hand, and those who only perceive particulars or intelligibles in their sleep, on the other.

There is finally a class of mentally disturbed or mad people whose humor and imaginative powers have become so corrupted that they see, whether in their sleep or waking state, things fabricated by their imaginative powers for which there is no equivalent in reality.[32]

This is how al-Fārābi attempts to explain those para-natural phenomena, such as dreams, prognostication (*kahānah*), vision (*ru'ya*)

31. Ibid., p. 94.
32. Ibid., p. 95.

and the prophetic office (*nubuwwah*), which is for him the highest stage attainable by humankind, through the use of the imaginative faculty. It is true, nonetheless, that what raises this faculty to the highest pitch of 'prophesying divine things' is the Active Intellect, which imparts to it the power to perceive present and future particulars or their similitudes, as well as the similitudes of immaterial intelligibles or other 'noble entities', by which al-Fārābi obviously meant angels and the like.[33]

This skillful interpretation was not well-received by al-Fārābi's Muslim successors, such as Ibn Sīna, who saw in it a derogation of the prophetic office, as a predicate of the somewhat subordinate faculty of the imagination. For Ibn Sīna and his followers, prophethood is rather a function of that part of the intellect which he calls 'holy reason' (*'aql qudsi*) and which is intermediate between potential and actual reason and is really a species of habitual reason (*'aql bi'l-malakah*). Once this habitual reason is actualized, it attains the level of acquired reason (*'aql mustafād*), the highest intellectual stage attainable by humankind.[34] However, it is to the credit of al-Fārābi that he recognized that an important part of the prophetic function, including the representation of particular occurrences, present or future, can be ascribed only to the imagination, rather than reason, whose domain is exclusively the universal.

33. Cf. ibid., p. 94.
34. Cf. Ibn Sīna, *Kitāb al-Najāt*, p. 206.

7

Ethical Theory

The attainment of happiness

The ultimate goal of human endeavor, as al-Fārābi asserts repeatedly, is happiness (*sa'ādah*), which in the *Nicomachean Ethics* Aristotle calls *endaimonia*, which they both identify with the contemplative life. The means of attaining this goal, as al-Fārābi states in the *Attainment of Happiness* (Taḥsīl al-Sa'ādah), are four, which he labels the four virtues, or rather four types of virtue: the theoretical, the reflective (*fikriyah*), the ethical and the political.[1]

Theoretical virtues, we are told, consist of 'those sciences whose ultimate goal is to gain certain knowledge of existing entities as intelligibles only'. Those sciences are of two types: 1) the primary sciences whose objects are known intuitively without effort or exertion and consist of the first principles of knowledge, and 2) those cognitions which are acquired through learning and instruction and require sustained investigation and reflection.

The objects of the second group of sciences are originally unknown, but through investigation or instruction become known as beliefs, opinions or scientific propositions. However, it is not always possible to

1. *Taḥsīl al-Sa'ādah*, p. 49.

achieve certainty in every case, but only conjecture (*ẓann*), conviction or imagination, since we are sometimes misled or are in error.[2] Those sciences cover the whole range of the Aristotelian syllabus, starting with logic and ending with metaphysics, which culminates in the knowledge of the ultimate causes of things and their Ultimate Principle, or God, who is 'the First Principle of all existing entities – by whom, from whom and for whom they all exist'.[3]

When humans attain the highest stage of theoretical knowledge, they will have attained the stage of union with the Active Intellect, the storehouse of all intelligibles. This stage al-Fārābi sometimes calls conjunction (*ittiṣāl*), sometimes proximity (*qurb, muqārabah*), in which humans' ultimate happiness consists.[4] At that point humans become, according to al-Fārābi, intellects in themselves and from being material beings (*hayūlāni*), they become divine beings (*ilāhi*). Al-Fārābi goes so far as to identify the Active Intellect, with which humankind is now conjoined, with the Qur'anic Faithful Spirit (*al-Rūh al-Amīn*) or Gabriel (*Jibril*) and the Holy Spirit (*al-Rūh al-Qudsi*).[5]

Al-Fārābi dwells on this divine or semi-divine goal of happiness in a number of works, including the aforementioned *Attainment of Happiness*, *Direction to the Path of Happiness* (*al-Tanbīh 'ala Sabīl al-Sa'ādah*) and others. And although a primary means of attaining this goal is theoretical, al-Fārābi does not ignore the many practical means, or moral virtues contributing to this good. This constitutes the substance of his ethical theory.

The moral virtues and their acquisition

Of human actions, al-Fārābi argues, some are deserving of praise, some of reproach, some of neither. Those actions which contribute to human happiness are the first mentioned, which fall into three categories: 1) those requiring the use of bodily organs; 2) those which are attended by the emotions of pleasure, pain, fear, craving or jealousy; and 3) those which require rational discrimination, or the use of one's intellectual faculties.

2. Ibid., p. 50.
3. Ibid., p. 63.
4. Cf. *Al-Siyāsah al-Madaniyah*, pp. 79 and 36.
5. Ibid., p. 32.

A person, he goes on to explain, is reproached for those actions which are vile, and commended for those actions which are virtuous. Our power of rational discrimination (*tamyīz*) is reprehensible when we are unable to discriminate between right or wrong, or do so haphazardly and without conscious intent. It is only when the power of good judgment in us has become an ingrained habit (*malakah*), whereby we are able to discriminate between right and wrong instantly, that we are guarded against morally nefarious judgments and are launched on the path leading to happiness.[6] Thus, a good character and a sound power of discrimination between right and wrong are essential prerequisites of attaining happiness at the practical level.

Character, for al-Fārābi, consists in the ability to cultivate the disposition (*isti'dād*) of choosing the right and shunning the wrong willfully. Whether virtue is natural or acquired, then, can be answered by saying that humans are disposed by nature to acquire certain virtues or technical skills, but only when this disposition has become an ingrained habit in them are their actions described as virtuous or vicious. Aristotle actually lays down three conditions for the goodness or badness of action: knowledge, choice and a 'firm and unchangeable character' (*ethos*); hence the term 'ethics'. In other words, an isolated action, for him, is not described as right or wrong unless it emanates from a good or bad character.[7]

A chief characteristic of a virtuous person is moderation (*tawassuṭ*), defined as the ability to determine 'the time, the place, the agent, the patient, the origin and the instrument of the action as well as the reason for which the action is done'.[8] Virtuous actions are so regarded because of their moderate quality. They include: 1) courage, which is a mean between cowardice and foolhardiness (*tahawwur*); 2) generosity, which is a mean between 'squandering wealth', which is an excess, and niggardliness, which is a defect; 3) temperance, which is a mean between excessive pleasure-seeking and defective moral torpor; and 4) good cheer, which is a mean between the excess of playfulness and the defect of boorishness or insensitivity.

6. Cf. *al-Tanbīh 'alā Sabīl al-Sa'ādah*, p. 54.
7. Cf. *Nicomachean Ethics*, II, 1105 *a* 30f.
8. *al-Tanbīh*, p. 60.

These virtues might be described as moral or practical. Al-Fārābi gives, along Aristotelian lines, a parallel list of intellectual virtues, which includes: 1) wisdom, or the knowledge of the ultimate principles and causes; 2) practical reason, which corresponds to Aristotle's prudence (*phronesis*), already discussed; 3) reflection (*fikr*), or the ability to 'judge rightly and to discern those things which are best and most suited for what we are out to perform', as a means of attaining happiness or something else conducive to happiness;[9] 4) acumen (*kays*) or the power to discover what is best and most suitable for attaining certain subordinate goods; 5) cunning (*dahā'*) or the ability to determine what is most suited for attaining a supposed good, such as wealth, pleasure or noble social standing; and 6) duplicity or deceitfulness, as the ability to discover the most effective means to achieve a base goal, deemed to be good, such as easy gain or base pleasure.[10]

All these virtues, which are really subdivisions of practical reason, are simply means of attaining the goal, but are different from the ultimate goal which, for al-Fārābi, is nothing other than happiness.

Evil and not-being

As a prelude to the discussion of the nature of evil and its relation to being, al-Fārābi posits that being or existence admits of four subdivisions or realms:

1. What cannot possibly not exist; i.e. the necessary.
2. What cannot possibly exist; i.e. the impossible.
3. What cannot possibly not exist at a certain time; i.e. the probable.
4. What can equally exist as not exist; i.e. the possible or contingent (*jā'iz*).[11]

He then goes on to explain that the noblest and most perfect of these subdivisions is the first, i.e. the necessary (1); whereas the meanest and most imperfect is the contingent (4).

9. Ibid., p. 55.
10. Ibid., p. 58.
11. *Fuṣūl*, p. 78.

A second postulate he lays down is the Neoplatonic maxim that everything that exists, independently of human volition or choice, is good. Evil, by contrast, is of two types which are actually related to the human condition: a) misery (*shaqā'*), which is the antithesis of happiness, already shown to be the chief good, and b) whatever is conducive to misery. It consists of those voluntary actions that conduce to the greatest privation of happiness. It follows that both forms of misery or evil are voluntary, just like the forms of happiness or good corresponding to them. Thus, in the above realms, corresponding to the necessary, the probable and the contingent or possible, 'the good consists of the First Cause, whatever is a concomitant thereof or is a concomitant of what is a concomitant thereof up to the end of the series of necessary concomitants'.[12] It follows that no part of that series of concomitants admits of evil, 'since every such part exists in accordance with an order of just desert or merit [*isti'hāl*]',[13] and is accordingly good. In other words, every such part is good insofar as it is a logical consequence or concomitant of the First Cause, who is supremely good, or may be said to exist justly or in accordance with just desert.

Having asserted that evil can only be predicated of anything that exists on ethical or axiological grounds, as his use of the expression 'just desert' clearly suggests, al-Fārābi goes on to refer to those philosophers, by whom he probably meant the Neoplatonists in general, who identified good with being, pure and simple, and evil with not-being, pure and simple.[14] He seems to object to this view on the ground that that unqualified position does not take account of the moral criterion of 'just desert' he has proposed and of which the only other expositor I can think of is the Greek philosopher Heracleitus (*c.* 500 BCE), who conceived of a cosmic law of justice (*Dike* or *logos*) governing the world.[15]

Privation or not-being (*'adam*) is for al-Fārābi a form of imperfection peculiar to certain things, just as being in need of certain conditions for a thing to exist is an imperfection. Similarly, whatever has an opposite is

12. Ibid., p. 80.
13. Ibid., p. 81.
14. Ibid., p. 81.
15. Cf. Windelband, *History of Ancient Philosophy*, p. 54.

imperfect; since for it to exist, its opposite must cease to exist. What has no privation, therefore, has no opposite and what does not need anything external to itself in order to exist has no opposite. It follows, as we saw earlier, that God, who has no opposite, is not liable to privation or not-being and does not need anything external to Himself to exist, and, being both necessary and self-sufficient, must be perfect.

Evil, on the other hand, has no existence in any of the three worlds that exhaust the totality of existing things: 1) what is independent of matter, or the sum-total of the intelligible forms and higher spirits that make up the intelligible world; 2) the heavenly spheres, which, as we have seen, are incorruptible; and 3) material entities considered in themselves and regardless of considerations of 'just desert'. In other words, al-Fārābi appears to imply that, as such, material entities, or the material world in general, are morally neutral. Thus, in the intelligible and spiritual worlds, evil is excluded, on the ground that nothing happens in these worlds without desert or for a good reason. Even the heavenly spheres and the material world are excluded. For what happens for the most part, as probable, or for the least part, as contingent or possible, or for no reason, as fortuitous, actually happens according to a just order of desert or merit. Only in the realm of willful action, where material means are used, al-Fārābi contends, is good or evil to be found; good and evil will depend in such cases on the right use or misuse of those material means, rather than on their specific natures, which are morally neutral or indifferent.[16] Voluntary evil and voluntary good may thus be identified with wrong or right choice. Such choice is good when the will is rightly guided by the rational faculty, assisted by the lower faculties of sensation, imagination and desire, and is directed towards the supreme good, which is happiness; but is evil when the imagination or rational faculty is oblivious of this supreme good and the will is then directed towards inferior goods, such as pleasure or profit. Sometimes, one may apprehend true happiness as the chief good, but not pursue it with any keenness, and continue to seek the lower good instead. In that case, whatever results from one's actions will be evil.[17]

16. Ibid., p. 81.
17. Cf. *al-Siyāsah al-Madaniyah*, pp. 73f.

In practical terms, the moral teacher has a grave responsibility in dealing with moral infirmity, which is similar to the responsibility of the physician. When the physician has diagnosed the illness of the patient, as owing to an excess or defect of heat or other humors, he or she proceeds to regulate those humors according to the precepts of the art of medicine.[18] In like manner, when the moral teachers have determined that their moral charge has a tendency to choose wrong or evil actions, they will resort to any means necessary to restore the moral health of that charge, just as the physicians are concerned with restoring their patients' physical health. The health of the body, we are then told, consists in the temperance of its humors; that of the city, and by analogy that of the individual, in the temperance of its powers or affections, at the hands of the moral teacher in the former case, and that of the ruler in the latter case. The responsibility of both teacher and ruler consists in restoring to the soul of the individual or the fabric of the state the temperance or equilibrium of which their vile actions have robbed it.[19]

A potent factor in diverting the agent away from the good is the illusion that pleasure is the chief good, so that whatever conduces to pleasure is good and whatever conduces to pain is evil. Al-Fārābi, therefore, finds it necessary, as Aristotle did in the *Nicomachean Ethics*, VIII and IX, to discuss pleasure in relation to virtue or vice. He divides pleasure into sensuous or intellectual, immediate or tardy, readily known or obscure. The most readily known pleasures are the immediate pleasures, to which the vulgar are readily drawn, thus tending to choose those actions which lead to them. The truly freemen, by contrast, are those, who in seeking the good or avoiding the bad, will not attach any importance to the pleasure or pain attendant on the choice; but will choose an action for its own sake. To the category of such freemen, al-Fārābi opposes that of the 'beastly men', who have neither the power of good judgment nor the stamina (*'azīmah*) to carry out what good action calls for. The man who has the power of good judgment, but not the stamina, is called a slave by nature; whereas the man who has the stamina, but not the power of good judgment, may be either willing to listen to

18. Ibid., p. 64.
19. Cf. *Fuṣūl*, p. 24.

others' advice or not. If not, he is no better than the beastly man; but if willing to listen, he ceases to be slavish and is closer to the freeman.[20]

Al-Fārābi concludes this discussion by reiterating his grand thesis that the good is twofold: 1) knowledge for its own sake, and 2) knowledge coupled with action. That is why philosophy, we are reminded, has two subdivisions, theoretical and practical. Now, insofar as the determination of the virtuous actions that are the pre-conditions of happiness is the business of philosophy, by which al-Fārābi no doubt meant philosophy in its theoretical capacity, philosophy must necessarily be regarded as the means of attaining happiness. For it inculcates in its student that sound judgment without which the discrimination between good and bad actions is not possible.

Despite this pre-eminent role which al-Fārābi assigns to theoretical philosophy, as a guide to ultimate perfection or happiness, he concedes nonetheless that to attain the goal of uttermost perfection, three varieties of virtue or excellence are needed: theoretical, reflective and ethical, to which the practical arts should be added.[21]

Justice and friendship

The two moral virtues that figure most prominently in al-Fārābi's ethical scheme are friendship and justice. Friendship is either natural and instinctive or voluntary. Voluntary friendship is grounded in the community of virtue, advantage or pleasure, which brings people together; whereas natural friendship is grounded in the community of beliefs concerning the First Principle, or God, the spiritual entities, or angels, and that of pious individuals, who are the models for others to follow. This community, however, extends to beliefs pertaining to the origin of the world, humans and their relation to the higher, spiritual entities and is clearly part of the religious bond, which is, for al-Fārābi, the pre-condition of true happiness.[22] The bond of common (religious) beliefs and practices conducive to happiness is discussed in great detail in

20. *Tanbih*, p. 70.
21. Ibid., p. 77.
22. Cf. *Fuṣūl*, pp. 70f.

al-Fārābi's best known work, significantly entitled the *Opinions of the Inhabitants of the Virtuous City* (*al-Madīnah al-Fāḍilah*), and will be dealt with in the next chapter.

As for justice, al-Fārābi, like Aristotle, begins by distinguishing the various meanings of justice (*'adl*). There is first the equitable distribution of common goods and honors, consisting of security, property and social standing. Equitable distribution of such goods or honors, he states, should be proportionate to the recipient's merits; if it is in excess or defect, it ceases to be justice and turns into its opposite, or injustice.[23] There is another meaning of 'justice', which consists in 'man's use of his virtuous actions in relation to others, no matter what virtues are involved'.[24] This is the sense to which Aristotle refers in the *Nicomachean Ethics* as complete justice, or the fact that 'he who possesses it can exercise his virtue, not only in himself, but toward his neighbors also'.[25] The nature of justice as a political virtue, which regulates the relations of the citizens to each other and forms the core of Plato's *Republic*, will be discussed in the next chapter.

23. Ibid., p. 71.
24. Ibid., p. 74.
25. *Nicomachean Ethics*, V, 1128 *b* 30.

8

Political Theory

The principles of political association

As already mentioned, the paramount standing of al-Fārābi in the history of Islamic philosophy is threefold: as a logician, a metaphysician and a political philosopher. In the last respect, he has hardly an equal. Even philosophers who wrote on political theory, such as Ibn Bajjah (d. 1138) and Averroes (d. 1198), were thoroughly indebted to him.

After laying down the metaphysical and cosmological groundwork of his Neoplatonism, al-Fārābi proceeds to discuss the principles of political association in the *Virtuous City* and the *Civil Polity*. In both treatises, he starts from the premise that humans cannot attain the perfection they are destined to attain, outside the framework of political association. For, they are constantly in need of the assistance of their fellows in the provision of their basic needs and their very survival. Thus arise the three types of association: the large, identified with the world at large (*ma'mūrah*, *oikiomene*), the intermediate, identified with the nation (*ummah*), and the small, identified with the city-state (*madīnah*, *polis*). Against these three perfect forms of political association are then set the three imperfect forms of large, intermediate and small.[1]

1. Cf. *Al-Madīnah al-Fāḍilah*, p. 96 and *al-Siyāsah al-Madaniyah*, pp. 69f.

Now, political association can be directed towards the attainment of true happiness, on the one hand, or towards certain contrary goals, such as pleasure or the acquisition of wealth. Thus arise the virtuous city and the corresponding virtuous associations, as against the non-virtuous cities and the corresponding non-virtuous associations, in which misery, ignorance and depravity (*fisq*) thrive.[2]

The virtuous city is then compared by al-Fārābi to a sound body, whose organs cooperate in ensuring the health of the animal, as well as its survival. Like the body, whose organs differ in rank or function, the parts of the city differ in rank and function, too. Hence, just as we find in the former a master organ, which is the heart, subserved by other, lower organs, we find in the latter a human master (*ra'īs*), served by subordinates, who carry out his orders. These subordinates are in turn served by other subordinates until we reach the lowest category of subordinates who are not served by anybody. The basic difference between the organs of the body and the parts of the city, al-Fārābi explains, is that the actions of the former are natural, whereas the actions of the latter are voluntary.

The master organ and the master ruler (ra'īs)

Al-Fārābi proceeds next to characterize the chief ruler of the city, who corresponds to the heart, or master organ of the body, as the supreme manager of the affairs of the city, or its head. This ruler may be compared to the First Cause, who presides over immaterial entities, beneath which lie the heavenly bodies, followed by material entities. All inferior entities follow and imitate the higher, culminating in the highest, who is the First Cause.

The two essential qualifications of the chief ruler are the natural disposition or aptitude to rule, coupled with voluntary traits or habits suited for that purpose. Like the First Cause, the chief ruler of the virtuous city is then characterized as one who possesses full intellectual perfection, as both subject and object of thought (*'āqil, ma'qūl*). In addition, he is one in whom the imaginative faculty has reached the highest pitch, whereby he is able to receive from the Active Intellect the knowledge of particulars, in either themselves or their likenesses, as well as that of

2. Ibid., pp. 109f.

intelligible forms. At that point, the ruler is able to achieve the condition known as the acquired intellect (*'aql mustafād*), which is the highest intellectual stage attainable by humankind. This condition is labeled by al-Fārābi proximity (*muqārabah*) to the Active Intellect,[3] called elsewhere conjunction (*ittiṣāl*).

If this intellectual condition is conjoined to the imaginative faculty, its bearer becomes a recipient of revelation from God, who transmits His messages to him through the intermediary of the Active Intellect, first as intelligible and later as imaginative forms. Thus, he becomes by virtue of what his passive intellect receives a perfect philosopher, sage (*ḥakīm*) or rational human (*muta'aqqil*), and by virtue of what his imaginative faculty receives, a prophet, who is called upon to warn about future events or inform about present particulars.[4] The man in whom these conditions are fulfilled, concludes al-Fārābi, is worthy of the office of chief ruler, since he is able, better than anybody else, to identify every action conducive to happiness and guide others to true happiness and the actions leading to it.[5]

*The qualifications of the chief ruler (*ra'īs*)*

Al-Fārābi then goes on to list the qualifications or attributes of the chief ruler in a somewhat utopian manner. Such a ruler, who is not subject to any higher person, he asserts, should be regarded as the Imām or head of both the virtuous city and the world at large (*al-ma'mūrah*). Here, al-Fārābi appears to be thinking of the Sunnite caliph, who ruled the whole of the Islamic world or the Abode of Peace (*Dār al-Salām*); although in current usage, the term 'Imām' was usually reserved for the spiritual and political head of the Shi'ite community.

Firstly, the chief ruler should be sound of body and limb, so as to be able to perform every function he chooses with great facility.

Secondly, he should be by nature capable of good understanding and grasp of whatever he is told, according to the intent of the speaker.

3. Ibid., p. 103.
4. This is a reference to the double role assigned to the Prophet in the Qur'an, as a bearer of good or bad news (*mundhir* or *bashīr* and *nadhīr*).
5. Cf. *al-Madīnah*, p. 704.

Thirdly, he should be endowed with a good power of retention of what he understands, sees, hears or perceives.

Fourthly, he should be intelligent and quick-witted, so as to grasp the import of any proof as it is given.

Fifthly, he should be eloquent and his tongue pliant in articulating fully whatever he wishes to express.

Sixthly, he should be a lover of learning, fully receptive of instruction, not deterred by the pain attendant on it or the exertion it calls for.

Seventhly, he should not be a glutton in matters of food, drink or sex, detesting play by nature and shunning the pleasures it gives rise to.

Eighthly, he should be a lover of truth and its adepts, and a hater of falsehood and its adepts.

Ninthly, he should be magnanimous and a lover of honor, who detests by nature whatever is shameful.

Tenthly, he should have no interest in money and the fleeting goods of the world.

Eleventh, he should by nature be a lover of justice and a hater of injustice; fair in dealing with the oppressed and quick to respond to the call for redress.

Twelfthly, he should be firm in his resolve to do what he deems right, daring and brave.[6]

Al-Fārābi, who unquestionably adopted, as the model of his *Virtuous City*, Plato's *Republic*, has followed his lead in characterizing the chief ruler, but has invested him with prophetic qualities in addition to Plato's philosophic traits. A comparison of the two lists given in the *Republic* and the *Virtuous City* will reveal the measure of agreement or disagreement of the two philosophers.

To begin, Plato asserts that the philosopher-king should have a 'constant passion for any knowledge that will reveal [to him] something of that reality which endures forever',[7] by which he obviously meant the World of Ideas, corresponding to al-Fārābi's intelligible world. (This quality corresponds to a large extent to al-Fārābi's sixth quality or trait.)

6. Ibid., pp. 105f.
7. *Republic*, VI, 484 *b*.

The philosopher-king should also be a lover of truth and a hater of falsehood (al-Fārābi's eighth quality). He should be temperate and no lover of money (tenth quality). He should be brave; indeed, 'for such a man', as Plato puts it, 'death will have no terrors'[8] (corresponding to al-Fārābi's twelfth trait). He should be fair-minded, gentle and easy to deal with (al-Fārābi's eleventh quality). He should be quick to learn and to possess a vivid memory (al-Fārābi's third trait).

The three traits that appear to be missing in Plato's list are eloquence (5), sound bodily constitution (1) and love of justice (11), which specifically formed part of the qualifications for the caliphal office. As given by al-Māwardi in his *Political Ordinances* (*al-Ahkām al-Ṣulṭāniyah*), the seven conditions or prerequisites (*shurūt*) the caliph should meet to qualify for the caliphal office are: justice, knowledge, soundness of the organs of sense (including hearing, sight and speech), soundness of body, soundness of judgment, courage and finally the Quraysh pedigree.[9]

If these traits, which the chief ruler should possess, according to al-Fārābi, cannot be found in one individual, as Plato also conceded, but are found in more than one who possess the chief trait of wisdom, they would collectively qualify as rulers. If, on the other hand, wisdom is found in one, the second, third, fourth, fifth and sixth traits, mentioned above, in a series of others, they would all qualify to serve as rulers, provided they are all compatible in character. However, if wisdom is not found in any of the six, the city will be condemned to remain without a head and will be destined in time to perish.[10]

The virtuous city

The virtuous city, over which the chief ruler or Imām should preside, is represented by al-Fārābi as the political framework for the attainment of humankind's ultimate goal of happiness. Its inhabitants are held together by a community of purpose, both theoretical and practical. Accordingly, they should seek in the first place the knowledge of the First Cause and

8. Ibid., VI, 485 *c*.
9. Cf. *al-Ahkām al-Ṣulṭāniyah*, p. 6. The last qualification was rejected by the Kharijites and other political sects.
10. Cf. *al-Madinah al-Fāḍilah*, cf. *Republic*, 499 and 540.

all its attributes, and in the second place that of the immaterial forms (or intelligibles), as well as that of the 'spiritual' entities (or intellects), their properties, their actions and their ranks, ending in descending order with the Active Intellect. Next, the inhabitants of the virtuous city should seek the knowledge of the heavenly bodies and their properties, followed by the physical bodies, how they come into being and pass away and how whatever happens in the world of generation and corruption happens according to the principles of masterly production (*iḥkām*), justice and wisdom, wherein there is no imperfection or injustice.

Next, they should seek the knowledge of humans, how they are generated and how their faculties develop and are finally illuminated by that light which emanates from the Active Intellect and is the warrant of their apprehending the first principles on which all knowledge depends.

Other subjects with which the inhabitants of the virtuous city should be conversant are then given as: 1) the nature of will and choice; 2) the characteristics of the chief ruler and his subordinates; 3) the nature of revelation (*waḥy*) and how it is possible; 4) the nature of happiness; and 5) the fate of the non-virtuous cities (to be discussed later) and how those inhabitants are destined, after death, to suffer eternal damnation or total annihilation.[11]

Of the two modes of knowledge open to the inhabitants of the virtuous city – purely intellectual or abstract, and imaginative or representational – the privileged class of philosophers (*ḥukamā'*) achieve the former type by recourse to demonstration and intuition; whereas the public achieves it by recourse to representations (*mithālāt*), which are debased imitations of the demonstrations of the philosophers. Al-Fārābi refers to a third, intermediate class who question the representations of the masses and may be said to belong to the class of 'imitators of the philosophers', by which al-Fārābi probably meant the Mutakallimun, who partake of the inferior art of dialectic (*jadal*).[12]

However, this intermediate class whose members are concerned to defend their respective religions (*sing. millah*) are unable to grasp the demonstrations of the philosophers or the intelligibles with which they

11. Cf. *al-Madīnah al-Fāḍilah*, p. 121.
12. Ibid., p. 123 and *Kitāb al-Burhān*, p. 20.

are concerned. Therefore, they continue to cling to the images (*rusūm*) of the intelligible or the imprints of those images in their souls.[13]

The non-virtuous cities

Having outlined the virtuous city, its goals, the qualities of its chief ruler, and his pre-eminence as philosopher, Imām and prophet, al-Fārābi proceeds next to outline the variety of non-virtuous cities, which he designates as opposites (*muḍāddāt*) of the virtuous city, and how they differ from the original prototype.

There are, according to him, four generic types of non-virtuous cities: the ignorant,[14] the wayward (*ḍāllah*), the depraved (*fāsiqah*) and the renegade (*mubadillah*).[15] To these four categories is added in the *Civil Polity* the class of parasites or outgrowths, who may be compared to weeds, since they grow on the periphery of political life and contribute little to it. This anti-social class is followed by a 'beastly' class, which consists of people who resemble 'human beasts' or wild animals. Some of them live in woods, in isolation or in groups, copulate like wild beasts and feed on raw meat and vegetables, or hunt for their prey like fierce animals. They might be found at the extremities of the inhabited world, either the extreme south or the extreme north. Such people, al-Fārābi observes, should be treated like wild animals. If they can be put to human use, they should be assimilated; if not, and they prove to be useless or even dangerous, they should be treated like dangerous animals.[16] The same applies to dealing with their offspring.[17]

Of the four generic types of non-virtuous cities, the ignorant city or city of ignorance is clearly the worst. It is defined by al-Fārābi as one whose inhabitants have never known true happiness or even imagined it. Were they to be informed about it, they would not understand it or believe in it. The only goods they have grown up to value are those 'supposed' goods, such as having a sound body, wealth and pleasure, or

13. Cf. *al-Siyāsah al-Madaniyah*, p. 86. Cf. Kitāb al-Millah, p. 45.
14. *al-Jāhilah*. A more accurate reading is *jāhiliyah*, commonly used to refer to pre-Islamic or pagan times in Arabia.
15. Cf. *al-Madīnah al-Fāḍilah*, p. 109; *al-Siyāsah al-Madaniyah*, p. 87.
16. Al-Fārābi does not specify how, but does not appear to exclude their extermination.
17. Cf. *al-Siyāsah al-Madaniyah*, p. 87.

being fancy-free, and held high in popular esteem. The opposites of those alleged goods are identified by them with misery.[18]

The generic type of non-virtuous city, essentially deficient in the knowledge of the true good or real happiness, is then divided into six species: the necessary city (or city of necessity), the city of ignominy (*nadhālah*), the city of baseness (*khissah*), the city of honor (*karāmah*), the city of conquest and the democratic city (*janā'iyah*).

The city of necessity is defined by al-Fārābi as one in which people are content to seek the necessities of life, essential for the survival of the body, such as food, drink, shelter, raiment and sex.[19] The inhabitants of this city are willing to seek the necessities of life by recourse to various means, such as husbandry, tending cattle, hunting and even highway robbery, either openly or in secret. However, the most highly regarded among them is the most resourceful in acquiring those necessities by trickery or craftiness. Their leader is one who has mastered those arts and is able to provide those necessities or keep them for the citizens, even if he has to draw on his own personal resources.[20]

The city of ignominy is defined as one whose inhabitants are engaged in the accumulation of wealth from whatever source, not as a means to anything else, but rather as an end in itself. The most highly respected among them is the richest and most successful in accumulating wealth by devious means.

The base city, which has a certain similarity to the previous one, is one whose inhabitants are engaged in pursuing the pleasures of food, drink and sex, not for the sake of survival, but each for its own sake. This city is regarded as the happiest and most envied by the 'people of ignorance' (*jāhiliyah*), since its inhabitants are assured of the necessities of life and the means of leading a life of fun and games to the highest degree.[21]

The city of honor or timocracy (as Plato called it) is different; since the aim of its inhabitants is to be honored and admired, not only by their

18. Cf. *al-Madīnah al-Fāḍilah*, p. 109.
19. Ibid., p. 110. Plato refers briefly to this primitive state, where the primary concern is the provision of the necessities of life. Cf. *Republic*, II, 369 *d*.
20. Cf. *al-Siyāsah al-Madaniyah*, p. 88.
21. Ibid., p. 89. The term *jāhiliyah* often used here has some relation to the conventional use of the term as applied to pre-Islamic times.

own compatriots, but by the world at large. Such honor is lavished on them on account of either some significant achievement or nobility of descent (*ḥasab*), added to wealth, provided the honored person is willing to share his advantages with his compatriots. When this honored person is fully deserving of popular recognition on account of his wealth or noble ancestry, he will be rightly acknowledged as the leader or king. The best such rulers or kings are those who do not seek pleasure or wealth, either for themselves or their subjects, but seek honor, glory and praise, and thus become illustrious during their lifetime and after their death. Such rulers or kings will recognize merit wherever it is found and will appoint their worthy subjects to various positions or offices according to their merits.

Al-Fārābi dwells at length on the merits of the city of honor or timocracy, which, like Plato, he regarded as the nearest to the virtuous or perfect city. Sometimes, he observes, the love of honor and glory may be pushed to extremes and the ruler will then begin to squander the public treasure on lavish expenditures – sumptuous palaces, dress and royal emblems – and will strive to secure the royal succession for his children or grandchildren. At this point, the city of honor degenerates into the city of conquest or tyranny.[22]

What distinguishes the latter kind of city is that the sole aim of its inhabitants is conquest for its own sake and the pleasures attendant upon conquest. This goal, al-Fārābi explains, is common to the inhabitants of all the 'ignorant' cities. Some seek conquest for the sake of the money, blood or liberty of the conquered. The means used in the process may be treachery or open warfare. However, some conquerors will refuse to seize the property of the enemy when they are asleep or otherwise occupied. They vie with each other in the number of conquests, the instruments used or the endurance shown in warfare. As a result, they become so hardened and cruel that they are marked by 'quickness of anger, love of luxury, gluttony in the consumption of food and drink, sexual excess and competition for all otherworldly goods'.[23]

This city, which may also be called the predatory city, has two subdivisions:

22. Ibid., p. 94.
23. Ibid., p. 95.

1. The first is that whose sole aim in either conquest, even if such conquest does not accrue in any advantage to the conqueror, or competition for some 'base objects', which al-Fārābi does not name, but adds 'as reported about some Arabs', by which he probably meant the desert bedouin who were involved in constant tribal warfare for the sake of booty.
2. The second is that whose inhabitants aim at conquest for the sake of things they deem valuable, but for the sake of which, if they can secure them without violence, they will not resort to violence except where a highly desirable object is at stake. If they are assured of gaining such a desirable object without violence, through outside assistance or independently, they will abandon that object out of a sense of magnanimity. That is why such people are regarded as high-minded or brave.[24]

The democratic city, by contrast, is one whose inhabitants accord freedom the highest esteem and believe that everybody should be allowed to satisfy his desires without being hindered in any way. They also subscribe to the view that they are all fully equal and no one has any superior merit over others. Freedom in this city, verging on lawlessness, eventually generates a variety of perverse traits, pursuits and desires, leading ultimately to widespread division and chaos.

Although in such a city there are no class distinctions, no ruler or ruled, the most highly admired among its citizens are those who safeguard their freedom and are able to attain their private goals or satisfy their various desires. It may happen, however, that a citizen of this city is acknowledged as the rightful ruler of the state, due to his role in providing for the citizens' needs. He will be honored and respected by his subjects, but still continue to be regarded as their equal, even if he happens to have received his authority from his noble ancestors. Despite this distinction, such a ruler will continue to be subject to the will of the public (*jumhūr*), like everyone else.[25]

24. Ibid., p. 97.
25. Hence, the term *jumhūriyah* for 'republic' in current Arabic usage. Cf. *al-Siyāsah al-Madiniyah*, p. 100.

Although al-Fārābi, as we have seen, assigns the democratic city to the category of 'ignorant' cities, he concedes that it is 'of their cities, the admired and happy one'.[26] Viewed from the outside, he says, it looks like a garment covered with colorful figures and is sought after by any one who seeks to satisfy any of his desires. Thus, nations are drawn to it, and will inhabit it and contribute to its greater glory. In time, there arises in it a generation of youngsters who are different in nature or upbringing; and then it is duplicated on a large scale. It is even possible in time for people of virtue to be found in it, such as philosophers, orators and poets of every stripe. In fact, it may yield elements that enter into the constitution of the virtuous city.

Here al-Fārābi may be accused of a certain degree of vacillation. For, having assigned the democratic city to the category of ignorant cities, he now makes this qualified concession, which sounds strange. It is possible, of course, that he is simply reflecting in this respect the sentiments of Plato, who was one of the arch-enemies of democracy in ancient times but made a similar concession in its favor. For, despite its faults and the fact that it was far removed from his political ideal of aristocratic kingship, Plato refers to democracy in the *Republic* as a fertile ground for the emergence of every type of constitution. 'A democracy', he writes, 'is so free that it contains a sample of every kind and perhaps anyone who intends to found a state ... ought first to visit this emporium of constitutions and choose the model he likes best.'[27]

The other three subdivisions of non-virtuous cities – the depraved (*fāsiqh*), the renegade and the erring (*ḍāllah*) – differ in one important respect: their inhabitants have partaken of the knowledge of happiness, God, the Active Intellect and whatever the inhabitants of the virtuous city are supposed to know. Nevertheless, those inhabitants have in the process of time lost this knowledge or abandoned it, as is the case with the renegade city, or entertained false opinions regarding those matters, as is the case with the inhabitants of the erring city, or entertained sound beliefs, but acted in the same manner as the inhabitants of the ignorant rather than the virtuous city, as in the case of the depraved city.[28]

26. Ibid., p. 101.
27. *Republic*, VIII, 557 *b*.
28. Cf. *al-Madīnah al-Fāḍilah*, p. 111.

*The outgrowths (*nawābit*) as a hybrid class*

Finally, al-Fārābi refers, as already mentioned, to a peripheral class that clings to the actions of the virtuous city, but distorts or misunderstands them.[29] Some, whom he calls the 'hunters' (*mutaqqanisūn*) or 'opportunists', cling to the actions of the virtuous city, as a means not to happiness, but rather to something else, such as honor, wealth or positions of leadership. Others are drawn to the goals of the inhabitants of the ignorant city, but are prevented from seeking them by the laws of the city or its religion. Accordingly, they resort to the interpretation (*ta'wīl*) of the words of the lawgiver[30] or his ordinances in a manner that suits their fancies. This group is called the falsifiers (*muḥarrifah*). A third group of outgrowths will not seek deliberate falsification, but, owing to their ignorance and misunderstanding of the intent of the lawgiver, will interpret his words in a manner that does not accord with his intent. Then, their actions will be incompatible with the intentions of the chief ruler. This fourth group may be called the heretics (*māriqah*). Other similar groups are described by al-Fārābi as capable of 'imagining' the objects apprehended by the inhabitants of the virtuous city, but inclined to distort them. Some, however, are disposed to listen to the advice of those who might set their imaginings right and then are made to recognize the truth as it is. Some, on the other hand, are not so disposed, because they are drawn to the apparent goods sought by people of the ignorant city.

A fifth group *imagine* happiness and the first principles, but are not able to apprehend them, owing to their limited intelligence, and thus will never attain the rank of apprehending truth. As a result, they tend to suspect those who have attained that rank of being liars prompted by the desire for honor or conquest, or are simply moved by arrogance or self-conceit. They will then go so far as to imagine that all those who claim to know the truth are misguided and end up by succumbing to doubt in all things, professing accordingly that there is no certainty whatsoever. Those sceptics, al-Fārābi comments, are regarded as fools and ignoramuses by

29. Plato refers to a 'peripheral class' whom he compares to 'self-sown plants' in the *Republic*, VII, 520 *b*.
30. *Wāḍi' al-Sunnah*, which appears to refer to the Prophet.

philosophers and reasonable people. It is the duty of the ruler of the virtuous city, he comments, to pursue those outgrowths, attempt to reform them or drive them out of the city.[31]

A final group includes those who hold that the truth is what appears to anyone or is imagined to be the case, and accordingly that truth is a matter of conjecture (*ẓann*, *doxa*); and that even if there were such a thing as truth, it has not been attained yet. This appears to be a reference to the Sophists, to whom al-Fārābi refers in his *Philosophy of Plato.* Some of those Sophists go so far as to describe every alleged truth as a lie. However, some of them may be visited by such sadness or despondency, because of their inability to seek the truth, that they give up the search for truth altogether, in favor of the menial pursuits of the ignorant city, which they identify with happiness.[32]

Al-Fārābi concludes this discussion by declaring that those outgrowths, whom he compares to weeds, will never constitute a city or even a significant community, but will always be a peripheral fringe of the city. Whether al-Fārābi was thinking of the known heretics or non-conformists, generally referred to in Arabic sources as *Zindiqs*, we do not know. It is possible, of course, that he has in mind such notorious contemporary heretics as Ibn al-Rāwandi (d. 911) or his teacher, 'Īsa al-Warrāq (d. 909), when he speaks of those who engage in false or questionable 'interpretations' of the words or ordinances of the lawgiver (i.e. the Prophet).[33] He may even be thinking of his great contemporary, Abū Bakr al-Rāzi (d. *c.* 925), the great physician and philosopher, who stands out as the greatest non-conformist in Islam.[34]

Lawlessness and discord

Conceived under the sign of knowledge and virtue, the virtuous city, as we have seen, is dedicated to the goal of recognizing humans' position in

31. Cf. *al-Siyāsah al-Madaniyah*, p. 106.
32. Ibid., p. 107.
33. Ibid., p. 104.
34. Cf. M. Fakhry, *A History of Islamic Philosophy*, pp. 94f. The term *zindiq* or 'heretic' was applied in the Arabic sources to a large number of scholars or political leaders, such as the literary master Ibn al-Muqaffa', members of the Bannakid family, the poet Ba'shshār and the Umayyad Caliph Marwān II. Cf. Ibn al-Nadim, *Kitāb al-Fibrist*, pp. 486f.

the universe as rational animals searching for happiness and truth. Thus, al-Fārābi closes with a series of reflections on the plight of the inhabitants of the non-virtuous cities. To begin with, they are thoroughly confused and dispirited. Having observed that the law of the universe is one of conflict and opposition and that animals and humans prey on each other, sometimes for no avail, they have concluded that the conqueror always seeks to destroy or enslave the vanquished because he is convinced that the very existence of the vanquished is inimical to his own.

Moreover, since there is no order or justice in the world, war or conquest is perfectly justified according to them. For in the end the mightiest is the happiest, since there is no bond of friendship or social affinity between people, whether by will or by nature. If people must get together and work together, it can only be for a while or as long as need or necessity justifies it.[35] For the 'solitary' (*mutwaḥḥid*) cannot attend to their needs without the assistance of others, and this is how social association (*ijtimā'*) is justified.

To this pragmatic view of political association is opposed a genetic view, according to which the social bond is rooted in kinship or marital relations. Or it may be rooted in the recognition that submission to the will of the chief ruler, who provides for the needs of his subjects and safeguards their security against invasion, is the wise thing to do.

A further view regards the social bond as the by-product of community of character, national traits or language, holding the nation (*ummah*) together. Still others regard it as the by-product of neighborly contiguity or community of interest in matters of food, drink, trade or pleasurable pursuits, as in certain forms of geographic or economic association.[36]

Political justice and religious piety

In line with these views of social or political association, al-Fārābi goes on to consider what, according to some, is regarded as 'natural justice'. Commenting on what was the ancient Sophists' view of justice as the

35. Cf. *al-Madīnah al-Fāḍilah*, p. 128.
36. Ibid., p. 130.

advantage of the strongest, outlined in the first book of Plato's *Republic*,[37] he explains that, according to this view, justice is rooted in warfare or conquest (*taghālub*). The objects of such warfare or strife are the aforementioned goods sought by the inhabitants of the ignorant city; namely, security, honor, wealth and pleasure. Thus, according to this view, the subjugation of the vanquished by the conqueror is just and his actions are synonymous with virtue.

It may happen, however, that as a result of prolonged warfare, both sides, whether individuals or states, are forced to reach an accommodation. Under the terms of this accommodation, the two former warring parties will agree to split the booty and undertake not to contest the right of either side to dispose of it. These terms are compared by al-Fārābi to the terms of commercial exchange. Such accommodation will last so long as the two sides are of equal strength; but when the balance of power is disturbed, the accommodation will be violated and the two sides will revert to the law of conquest, unless they are threatened by an external aggressor who cannot be repulsed unless the two sides join ranks.[38] The consequent temporary alliance will last so long as the external danger persists; but when one side senses that it has the upper hand and the danger of external aggression has abated, it will revert to its old ways of confrontation or warfare.

If this state of affairs lasts for any length of time and neither side has the upper hand, people are led to believe that that the *status quo* is just, little realizing that it owes to weakness or fear.[39] Al-Fārābi appears to regard this view of international relations as natural, but not necessary.

Some people, he goes on to say, resort to religious devices to achieve the goals of conquest or ascendancy. They appeal to piety (*khushū'*) in seeking these aims, by professing belief in a Deity who manages the affairs of the world providentially (*yudabbir*), assisted by spiritual entities (i.e. angels), who superintend all human actions. This belief is supplemented by the practice of glorifying the Deity through prayers and incantations

37. Cf. *Republic*, I, 338 *c*. This was the view of the Sophist Thrasymachus, mentioned in al-Fārābi's *Philosophy of Plato*.
38. Cf. *al-Madīnah al Fādilah*, p. 134.
39. Ibid., p. 134.

(*tasābīh*). It is then held that whoever practices such rituals and renounces the coveted goods of this world will be rewarded by much greater good in the after-life. If, however, one does not, but continues to cling to worldly goods, one will be punished severely in the hereafter.

This is how al-Fārābi appears to interpret the rise of religion and religious institutions. He shows no sympathy for the practices of religious leaders or communities. For, as he comments, those practices are mere tricks or devices intended to achieve victory over the opponent. They are resorted to when other means have failed, and are practiced by those who are no longer able to achieve their goals by recourse to open warfare. In calling for the renunciation of worldly goods, they wish to give the impression that they are not really interested in them. Thus, they are trusted by others and their conduct is described as divine. Even 'their attire and looks', al-Fārābi adds, 'appear to be those of people who are not interested in these [worldly] goods on their own account'.[40] As a result, they end up being honored and admired and will earn the love of their followers, who submit to them willingly. Like the beasts (*wuhūsh*) of the wild, al-Fārābi goes on, these religious opportunists will resort either to violent confrontation or to trickery in pursuit of their goals. By recourse to deception or trickery, they are in fact more successful in attaining those goals. For by pretending to renounce worldly goods out of a sense of piety, they end up beating everybody in the acquisition of honors, social station, wealth and pleasure. They will, in addition, earn the esteem of their fellows and continue to grow in (fake) wisdom and certainty.

By contrast, those who practice the above-mentioned ways out of genuine piety are regarded by the general public as 'misguided, confused, miserable, mad and deficient in intelligence'.[41] Nevertheless, some people will continue to show them signs of esteem, but only in jest. Others will encourage them to stick to that path, so that they may profit themselves from the worldly goods the latter have renounced.[42] All these, al-Fārābi comments, are the misguided views of the inhabitants of the city of ignorance.

40. Ibid., p. 136.
41. Ibid., p. 137.
42. Ibid.

Having described what may be termed the law of conquest, as well as the exploitation of religious piety for purposes of gain or the subjection of others, al-Fārābi proceeds to review other views of social association, or what he calls in this context the human bond (*ribāt*). One of these views is that strife is confined to one species fighting another species. Where one species (i.e. the human) is concerned, peace is the natural norm. However, it is not excluded that members of the human species should fight each other over what is useful, provided this is done by recourse to 'voluntary transaction'. In dealing with other non-rational species, or wild animals, however, the only recourse is violence or taming by force, since for such species the concept of voluntary transactions does not arise.

This pacifist account of human relations, as given by al-Fārābi, rests on the premise that strife or pugnacity (*taghālub*) is not natural to humankind. However, the 'natural group' or nation might be forced to confront external invasion in certain circumstances. To do so effectively, the nation is divided into two classes: 1) a fighting class (i.e. the army or military class), and 2) a negotiating class (i.e. the diplomatic class), which will try to resolve conflicts with other nations peacefully. For the fighting class will not engage in open warfare freely, but only if they are compelled to ward off the threat of outside aggression.[43]

Although none of these views of war and peace appears to be al-Fārābi's own view, since he constantly injects the paranthetic 'they said' (*qālu*) into the discussion, it is probable that he favored the last mentioned pacifist view. The views attributed to the non-virtuous or ignorant cities are all predicated on the premise that their inhabitants are deficient in knowledge or virtue; only the pacifist class are credited with the rational gift of discrimination between what is humanly natural and what is not, what is useful and what is not.

The fate of the soul after death

Not only in this life, but also in the life to come, the opposition of virtuous and non-virtuous cities persists and determines the fate of the soul after death. On the whole, as we have seen, there are two categories of goals sought by the inhabitants of those cities.

43. Ibid., p. 140.

The souls of the inhabitants of the virtuous city are susceptible of a progression in the attainment of perfection and virtue proportionate to their dissociation with matter. When these souls have attained the limit of such perfection, they will be able to dispense with matter altogether, and then they will continue to exist in a disembodied state. In that state of incorporeal existence, these souls are rid of all those accidents or affections associated with the body, such as motion or rest. However, al-Fārābi does not deny that those souls will be subject to some degree of variation contingent upon the humors and traits of the bodies they originally subsisted in; but since such variations are infinite, the conditions of the souls after death will be infinite also.[44] This is how al-Fārābi appears to resolve the problem of individual survival after death, although he adds cryptically that 'to understand the condition [of these souls] and to conceive of it is difficult and unusual'.[45]

By contrast, the souls of the inhabitants of the non-virtuous cities can never dispense with matter, since none of the primary intelligibles has been imprinted on them. Thus, if the matter in which they subsisted disintegrates at death, nothing remains except the forms of the various stages of that matter, ending up in the forms of the four elements. These elements can then pass through a cycle of transformations, or reincarnations, in the forms of humans or animals. When they reach the latter stage, these souls are doomed to perish altogether, as lions and other beasts are so doomed.[46]

Al-Fārābi then details the various fates to which the inhabitants of each state are subject. Those of the inhabitants of the depraved city, who received certain virtuous opinions, although they failed to live up to them, will find themselves in a distressing condition. For, by virtue of those opinions, they will be liberated from matter; but by virtue of their perverse actions, they will be subject to great distress, owing to the tension between the rational and sensuous parts of their souls, which is creditable, and the practical part, which is not. The rational part, having been rid of bodily sensation, will then experience the greatest pain, which

44. Ibid., p. 112.
45. Ibid., p. 113.
46. Ibid., p. 118.

will endure forever. This pain goes on increasing in proportion to the number of similar souls joining the throngs of depraved souls forever.[47]

The fate of the inhabitants of the erring cities is similar to that of the inhabitants of the ignorant cities; namely, final annihilation, with one exception. Whoever has caused those inhabitants to be led astray, in pursuit of some ignoble goal, will be condemned to lead forever the life of misery reserved for the people of the depraved city. The same is true of the inhabitants of the renegade city; they too will perish, like the inhabitants of the ignorant city. Whoever was the cause of their reneging will suffer the fate of depraved cities, too.

Finally, it may happen that some inhabitants of the virtuous city will be compelled to perform the depraved actions of the ignorant cities. To the extent those victims of compulsion continue to resent what they have been compelled to do, their souls will not be marked by the evil traits of the citizens of the depraved city. That is why they will not be harmed by depraved actions, unless they have been forced to live in the midst of the inhabitants of ignorant or depraved cities against their will.[48]

For al-Fārābi, the fate of the soul after death is determined in the last analysis by the degree of knowledge and virtue attained during its earthly career. Such souls as have remained deficient in knowledge or virtue will perish completely, or live in a state of eternal misery because of the conflict between the rational and the sensuous parts of their souls. This latter fate is reserved collectively for the inhabitants of the depraved city. The inhabitants of the virtuous city, by contrast, will survive in a disembodied condition, untroubled by the cares or tribulations of corporeal existence.

Al-Fārābi concludes by asking whether this corporeal existence, or the temporary association of soul and body in this world, is natural or not. He begins by discussing the view of those who believe that happiness or perfection is attainable only in the world-to-come, the pre-condition of which being a virtuous life in this world. For this reason, they hold that the present, terrestrial existence of the soul is not natural; it should instead aspire to a higher life after departing this world. The pathway of

47. Ibid., p. 120.
48. Ibid.

this otherworldly happiness or perfection, according to this view, is the practice of virtue.[49]

Others, we are told, have denied this claim, asserting that the soul's existence in this world is natural, but has been corrupted by false opinions or perverse actions. As a result, people have been so confused as to deny that humans are humans or that human action is human action, a clear reference to the Sophists and other sceptics who have questioned whether genuine knowledge is possible. In fact, those Sophists denied that existing entities, whether intelligible or sensible, have a fixed nature or property. It is possible, they held, for the same thing to be this thing or its opposite, or for three times three to be equal to nine or not. It is even possible for an infinite number of entities, intelligible or sensible, which have not been thought or perceived yet, to exist. Even what is supposed to be a necessary corollary (*lāzim*) of a certain statement or its action may be different, since the actual status of any entity or its correlatives is a matter of chance (*ittifāq*).

In broader terms, this view of the Sophists is represented by al-Fārābi as tantamount to asserting that it is possible for the same thing or its opposite to be true or false at the same time; that what we know today to be the case may not be the case tomorrow and what is deemed impossible today may prove to be possible tomorrow. For al-Fārābi, these relativistic views mark the death of wisdom (*ḥikmah*) or knowledge of any kind.[50] Like Plato, he appears to reject the view of the Sophist Protagoras that man is the measure of all things, 'of that which is that it is and that which is not that it is not'.[51] On the substantive issue of the nature of the soul and its relation to the body, al-Fārābi is in agreement with the Platonic view that the soul is the essence of humankind and that its association with the body corrupts it. Hence, only by repudiating this association and becoming liberated from the bondage of the body, as Socrates put it, will the soul be able to achieve the perfection it is destined to achieve.

Against this Socratic-Platonic view of the duality of soul and body, al-Fārābi then presents a 'naturalistic' view according to which the body is perfectly natural; it is the accidents or affections of the soul which corrupt

49. Ibid., p. 142.
50. Ibid., p. 148.
51. Plato, *Theaetetus*, 152 *a*.

it. It follows, as the Stoics taught, that it is through the mortification of the body and the stemming of the affections of anger, pleasure and the like that happiness is achieved. For such affections, they held, are the causes of such supposed goods as wealth, honor, pleasure and love of conquest, associated with the spirited and concupiscent parts of the soul, which should be kept in check by the rational part. After referring to the views of such ancient philosophers as Empedocles and Parmenides,[52] al-Fārābi quotes an ancient maxim given in the Arabic sources as 'Die voluntarily and then you will live naturally.' By voluntary death, al-Fārābi explains, is meant the suppression of the emotions of desire and anger and by natural death the separation of the soul from the body. Conversely, the ancients, he states, meant by 'natural life' perfection and happiness.

Among the ancient Neoplatonists, the latter view was that of Porphyry of Tyre (d. 303), who inclined towards mysticism, like his master, Plotinus. Al-Fārābi himself did not incline towards mysticism. Accordingly, it is not surprising that he should label all these otherworldly and mystical views as false and go on to claim that they have given rise to 'opinions which gave birth to various religions [*milal*] in many of the erring cities'.[53] What these religions are, we are not informed, but it is possible, as Richard Walzer has suggested in his translation of and commentary on the *Virtuous City*, that al-Fārābi may have been thinking of certain Christian and Manichean sects, especially those who advocated an ascetic life of self-mortification and contempt for the world.[54] However, al-Fārābi's famous predecessor, al-Kindi, listed the various definitions of philosophy proposed by the ancients. The third of these definitions reads as follows: 'They have also defined it from the standpoint of its action, saying: "It is the practice of death." Death for them is twofold: natural, consisting in the soul relinquishing the use of the body; the other being the mortification of the desires.' Al-Kindi then goes on to explain that the latter is the death they meant, since mortification of desire is the pathway to virtue.[55]

52. Empedocles (*c.* 444 BCE) referred to the generation and corruption of existing entities to two opposite forces, love and discord (*philia, neikos*); while Parmenides (*c.* 485 BCE) referred the opposition to warmth or heat.
53. Ibid., p. 144.
54. Cf. Walzer (trans.), *Al-Fārābi on the Perfect State*, pp. 500f.
55. *Rasā'il al-Kindi*, I, p. 172.

This last notion is thoroughly Socratic and is eloquently expressed in the *Phaedo*, where the chief occupation of the philosopher is declared to consist in freeing the soul from the bondage of the body. For, as Socrates put it, the true philosophers are those 'who make dying their profession';[56] so much so that 'if you see anyone distressed at the prospect of dying ... it will be proof enough that he is a lover, not of wisdom, but of the body'.[57] In fact, Socrates adds, such a person would be a lover of wealth or reputation, as al-Fārābi also states.

56. *Phaedo*, 67 *e*.
57. Ibid., 68 *c*.

9

Al-Fārābi and Music

We referred in Chapter 3 to al-Fārābi's great skill as a lute-player, as an instance of his versatility as a musician, in addition to his status as logician, political philosopher and metaphysician. Apart from this practical skill, he appears to have been profoundly interested in the theory of music as well. This is illustrated by the large number of musical treatises he is known to have written. These treatises include a voluminous work entitled the *Large Musical Treatise* (*Kitāb al-Mūsīqa al-Kabīr*), which has survived, a short treatise on rhythm, *Kitāb fī Iḥṣā' al-Īqā'*, as well as a *Treatise on Tuning* (*Kitāb fi'l Nuqra*) and a *Discourse on Music* (*Kitāb fi'l-Mūsīqa*).[1]

In the preface of the *Large Treatise on Music*, al-Fārābi explains that his aim is twofold: 1) to lay down the first principles of music, which he regards as part of the mathematical sciences;[2] and 2) to expound the views of the leading theorists who dealt with music, evaluate them critically and correct their errors.

In the *Enumeration of the Sciences* (*Iḥṣā' al-'Ulūm*), he explicitly refers to these two parts as the theoretical and practical. Practical music, he then goes on to state, is concerned with identifying the various melodies and the instruments used to produce them, which he subdivides into two – natural and artificial. The natural instruments include the larynx, the

1. Ibn Abī Usaybi'ah, *Uyūnal-Anbā*, p. 608. Cf. Farmer, *A History of Arabian Music*, pp. 175f.
2. Cf. *Iḥṣā' al-'Ulūm*, pp. 105f.

uvula and its components, and the nose; whereas artificial instruments include the flutes, lutes (*'īdān*, plural of *'ūd*) and the like.

Theoretical music, on the other hand, gives the rational causes of melodies, not insofar as they inhere in matter, or are produced by a given instrument, but insofar as they are generally audible, regardless of the instruments or objects from which they derive.[3]

The same themes are developed fully in the *Large Treatise*, where al-Fārābi defines the practical 'art' (*sinā'ah*) of music as the art of melodies (*alḥān*). Such melodies, he then goes on to explain, may consist of a variety of tunes properly arranged or a group of such tunes that acquire by convention a certain connotation. The first variety is more general and includes any tunes produced naturally by any object; whereas the second consists of 'human sounds used to express certain intelligible notions which serve as the means of communication'.[4] By the second variety, al-Fārābi appears to mean songs or musical performances in general.

Melody, he then explains, may take one of two forms. The first is inner, consisting of imagining the tune intended; the second is the disposition or skill of producing that tune through the hand or through the mouth. Hence, the instruments used are divisible into lutes or other percussion instruments and flutes or other wind instruments, respectively.[5]

Imagination plays, for al-Fārābi, a major role in the production of melodies, as well as the invocation of sensuous objects, present or absent. The aim of such melodies is often to induce the sensation of pleasure in the hearer, or simply the representation of images imprinted in the soul, as happens in the case of drawings and sensible figures or shapes, associated with the arts of painting and sculpture. The pleasure induced by musical melodies is analogous, according to al-Fārābi, to that which accompanies all forms of sensuous perceptions, which are always accompanied by the sensation of pleasure or its opposite. Here, al-Fārābi inveighs against the Pythagoreans, who refer such pleasure or pain to the influence of the celestial spheres.[6]

3. Cf. *Iḥṣā' al-'Ulūm*, pp. 105f. Cf. Shehadi, *Philosophies of Music in Medieval Islam*, p. 53.
4. *Kitāb al-Mūsīqa al-Kabīr*, p. 47.
5. Ibid., p. 52.
6. Ibid., pp. 64 and 89. Cf. Shehadi, *Philosophies of Music*, p. 54.

The production of melodies or the musical art in general is rooted, according to al-Fārābi, in those instinctive traits which are associated with the 'poetical instinct', as well as the 'animal instinct' which is rooted in the human desire for relief from exertion. That is why one does not perceive the passage of time when one is listening to music, since one is relieved of the anxiety attendant upon the consciousness of the flux of time. The appreciation or enjoyment of music does not necessarily require practical experience, as attested by the testimony of ancient philosophers, among whom al-Fārābi mentions Ptolemy, Themistius and Aristotle.[7]

The second volume of the *Large Treatise* deals with practical musical issues, such as the 'elements of the musical art', musical instruments and musical compositions. Here, al-Fārābi displays an amazing musical virtuosity, as illustrated by the detailed discussion of musical notation, which is of interest only to the practitioner of the art.

A large part of the second volume is concerned, however, with theoretical questions, such as the aim of music, which al-Fārābi regards as analogous to that of poetry, as already mentioned. Both consist, according to him, in aiming at humankind's ultimate happiness (*sa'ādah*), a principal theme of his ethics, as we have seen, as well as pleasurable sensations or enjoyment, whether constantly or at certain intervals. To appreciate fully the uses of musical compositions, one must first understand the uses of poetry and its many forms. The uses of the two arts, poetry and music, are then stated to belong to two inquiries, logic in the first case and politics in the second. Poetics, it will be recalled, formed part of the logical corpus, according to al-Fārābi. The determination of the uses or abuses of music, he appears to suggest, belong to the 'political art', which includes ethics.[8]

The correlation between poetry and melody is a central theme of al-Fārābi's. He describes melodies associated with poetry as the perfect type, as compared with those which are associated with compound objects of perception, such as visual, representative or decorative objects. For, of the two varieties, the poetical is particularly effective in 'inducing sound traits of character and compelling its hearers to perform creditable actions. It is not only useful in that respect, but also in cultivating those fine traits in

7. Ibid., pp. 102f.
8. Ibid., p. 1188.

the soul, such as wisdom and science, as was the case with the ancient melodies attributed to the Pythagorans.'[9] He lays down as a condition for such poetic effect the use of simple and pleasurable images and linguistic terms, instead of far-fetched terms, images or representations.

It is characteristic of poetical discourse, as Aristotle argued, to be concerned with what is possible in the absolute sense, whether natural or voluntary. Nevertheless, it can take one of two forms, serious or playful. The former include those forms of poetry which contribute to attaining the utmost happiness or point to it, whereas the latter contribute to relaxation or relieving pressure, as a prelude to serious endeavor. That is why, al-Fārābi states, Aristotle compares playful or comic poetry to salt in relation to food.[10]

Here, al-Fārābi comments on the attitude of religious laws (*shārāi'*), which he does not name, to playful or comic poetry and song. Because the public tends to identify pleasure and relaxation with genuine happiness, those laws have tended to prohibit them, as happens in the case of melodies in 'this our time and our countries'.[11] Although al-Fārābi is not explicit, he appears to be referring to the well-known Qur'anic strictures against poetry and the poets. Thus, Surah 26, verses 24–6 read: 'As for the poets, the perverse follow them. Do you not see that they wander aimlessly in every glen? And that they say what they do not do?' However, there is no mention in the Qur'an of melody or song; but the Prophetic Traditions (*Ḥadith*) abound with strictures against singing and singers; such as this tradition attributed to 'Aisha, wife of the Prophet: 'Verily, Allah has made the singing girl unlawful, and so He has made selling her and teaching her.' Another *ḥadith* reads: 'Satan [*Iblis*] was the first who wailed and the first who sang.' More damning is this *ḥadith*: 'Music and song cause hypocrisy to grow in the heart as water makes corn grow.'[12]

Despite these explicit censures in the *Ḥadith*, it is noteworthy that those traditions are counterweighed by a series of other traditions that are less explicit, and therefore more tolerant of singers and songs, of which

9. Ibid., p. 1181.
10. Ibid., p. 1185.
11. Ibid., p. 1187.
12. Cf. Farmer, *A History of Arabian Music*, p. 24.

Farmer gives a number.[13] Al-Fārābi, on the whole, appears to favor this tolerant attitude and does not dwell at length on the question of the Islamic law's attitude to poetry or song, whether in its rigid or its tolerant form. The fact that he wrote extensively on the subject of music would appear to show that he did not favor the scriptural prohibitions or censures against music and poetry.

13. Ibid., pp. 25f.

10

Al-Fārābi in History

The triumph of Neoplatonism

The fascination of Islamic Neoplatonism, of which al-Fārābi was the founder, stemmed from its profoundly religious, and to some extent, mystical appeal. This is illustrated by the way in which Ibn Sīna, al-Fārābi's spiritual disciple, interpreted it later in his life. In his so-called 'oriental philosophy' (*al-Hikmah al-Mashriqiyah*), his mystical tracts and especially his *Indications and Admonitions* (*al-Ishārat wa'l-Tanbīhāt*), Ibn Sīna deliberately went beyond the methods of Peripatetic philosophers in the direction of a mystical or 'illuminationist' (*Ishrāqi*) method, which the so-called *Ishrāqi* philosophers later developed in full. Of those philosophers, al-Suhrawadi (d. 1191) and al-Shirazi (d. 1641) were the principal exponents, whose debt to Ibn Sīna was very great.[1]

From a strictly metaphysical and cosmological standpoint, Neoplatonism appeared to safeguard the transcendence of the Qur'anic God, 'unto whom nothing is like' (Qur'an 42:9), on the one hand, and to give a rationally plausible interpretation of the origination of the world, on the other. This emanationist interpretation, it is true, proved later on to be irreconcilable with the Qur'anic concept of creation *ex nihilo* and in time;

1. Cf. M. Fakhry, *A History of Islamic Philosophy*, pp. 293f.

but had at any rate the merit of offering a rational account of such origination, which Aristotle, the Greek materialists and the naturalists, and even Hindu religionists had not entertained.

What further recommended Neoplatonism to Muslim philosophers and other scholars was its exalted concept of the soul in general and reason in particular. For, not only was reason the token of the ascendancy of humankind, created in 'God's image and likeness', as a Prophetic tradition has it, but also the pathway to the discovery of humankind's true happiness and destiny as citizens of the higher world. For, as Neoplatonism taught, it is by virtue of the soul's aspiration to be released from the bondage of the body and to rejoin the intelligible world to which it originally belonged, that humans will finally fulfill their destiny. The Qur'an, especially in the early Makkan surahs, underlined in graphic terms the fate in store for humankind on the Day of Judgment, and their eventual consignment to a life of everlasting misery or bliss in hell or paradise. This fate was inseparable in the end from the life individuals had led in this life as free and rational agents. In his own interpretation of humankind's fate, as we have seen, al-Fārābi appears to concede that the souls of the virtuous will survive the destruction of their bodies, but not the vicious or their leaders in the non-virtuous cities. The problem with which all the Muslim Neoplatonists struggled unsuccessfully was that of the resurrection of the body. That the soul was indestructible, according to them, was not in question, but al-Fārābi, Ibn Sīna and their followers continued to tread a dangerous path of vacillation or ambiguity. Committed to Plato's and Plotinus's sense of the utter separability of soul and body, the Muslim Neoplatonists had no problem in conceding the indestructibility of the former, but not that of the latter.

Al-Fārābi's philosophical legacy

All al-Fārābi's philosophical successors, with few exceptions, tended to endorse his concept of the transcendence of the Supreme Being or the One, the emanation of the intelligible and the material worlds from this Being, the nobility of reason, as the first-born of the One, so to speak, and the eventual return of the soul to its original abode in the higher world.

However, the philosopher who stands out as al-Fārābi's most articulate successor was Ibn Sīna, who acknowledges in his own autobiography his debt to his predecessor. Despite his unabashed self-confidence, Ibn Sīna admits in that autobiography, which he dictated to his disciple Abū 'Ubayd al-Juzjāni, that he read the *Metaphysics* of Aristotle forty times, but could not fathom the intent of its author until he lighted, at a book-dealer's shop, on al-Fārābi's book the *Intentions of Aristotle in his Metaphysics*, which he bought for a dew dirhams, went home and read. Thereupon, we are told, 'The intents of that book were revealed to me at once, since I had memorized it by heart.' He was so delighted, we are further told, that the next day he gave generously to the poor, in token of his gratitude to God.[2]

Al-Fārābi's extant tract bearing the title *Intentions of the Sage* [i.e. Aristotle] *in Each Chapter of his Book Called The Book of Letters*,[3] consists of a short list of the topics Aristotle dealt with in the *Metaphysics*, known in the Arabic sources as the *Book of Letters*, and could not have adequately served the purpose referred to by Ibn Sīna. However, it is possible that Ibn Sīna had access to a lost treatise of al-Fārābi which was more instructive. In fact, a treatise entitled the *Second Teaching* (*al-Ta'līm al-Thāni*) by al-Fārābi is mentioned by a late bibliographer, Hajji Khalifah (d. 1657) as the basis of Ibn Sīna's whole philosophy,[4] and may be the treatise of al-Fārābi which Ibn Sīna had in mind.

However, apart from this external evidence, the internal evidence fully confirms Ibn Sīna's profound debt to al-Fārābi. His own merit consists, on the whole, in the greater thoroughness of his exposition of the chief tenets of al-Fārābi's metaphysics, cosmology and psychology. His style is more fluent and is far less repetitive and rhapsodic than al-Fārābi's, who often tends to restate in almost identical terms the same points in some of his works, such as the *Virtuous City* and the *Civil Polity*. By contrast, Ibn Sīna tends to be more thematic in dealing with the major topics of his metaphysics, cosmology and psychology, as the titles of his major books clearly show.

2. Cf. Gohlman, *The Life of Ibn Sīna*, p. 34.
3. Cf. Arabic text in Dieterici, *Al-Fārābi's Philosophische Abhandlungen* pp. 34–8.
4. Cf. *Kashf al-Zunūn*, III, p. 98.

Accordingly, the emanationist worldview proposed by al-Fārābi, the transcendence of the One, called by Ibn Sīna the Necessary Being, the fate of the soul as a citizen of the intelligible world and the eventual conjunction of the acquired intellect with the Active Intellect form the fabric of Ibn Sīna's philosophy, just as they formed the fabric of al-Fārābi's.

As for the substantive points on which the two philosophers diverged, we might mention an interesting refinement on al-Fārābi's account of the various stages in the process of emanation. For Ibn Sīna, the first intellect is engaged in a triple act of apprehension, as against al-Fārābi's double. In the first instance, it apprehends its author, the Necessary Being, giving rise thereby to the second intellect. In the second instance, it apprehends itself as *necessary* through its author, giving rise thereby to the *soul* of the outermost sphere, as al-Fārābi also held. In the third instance, it apprehends itself as *contingent* in itself, giving rise thereby to the *body* of the outermost sphere[5] – a distinction that al-Fārābi did not make.

It was in psychology, however, that Ibn Sīna went well beyond al-Fārābi in developing a coherent system, which became the generally accepted psychological system in both East and West. His tabulation of the faculties of the soul is so thorough that Muslim moral philosophers, such as Miskawayh (d. 1037), al-Tūsi (d. 1274) and others, were thoroughly dependent on it. Even Scholastic, Latin philosophers, such as St. Thomas Aquinas (d. 1274) follow this tabulation faithfully. In that respect, Ibn Sīna outstripped in point of systematism Aristotle himself.

On some specific psychological points, Ibn Sīna diverges from the teaching of al-Fārābi in a significant way. For instance, al-Fārābi, it will be recalled, attributed to the imaginative faculty, the double role of prognostication or prophecy (*kahānah*) and that of receiving supernatural revelations or intimations, either in waking or in sleep.[6] This involved, as Ibn Sīna probably perceived, a certain derogation from the prophetic function, which he assigns instead to the higher faculty of reason. When reason attains the level of *habitual* reason (*bi'l-malakah in habitu*), he states, it sometimes takes the form of intuition (*ḥads*), whereby some gifted

5. Cf. *al-Najāt*, pp. 313f. and *al-Shifā'* (*Ilāhiyāt*), I, pp. 410f.
6. Cf. *al-Madīnah al-Fāḍilah*, p. 84.

individuals are able to achieve conjunction (*ittiṣāl*) with the Active Intellect almost effortlessly. This condition may be called, according to Ibn Sīna, holy reason (*'aql qudsi*), which imparts to the lower imaginative faculty certain sensible representations of events past or present, which are prognostic in character. However, the gift of prophecy, as such, is confined for Ibn Sīna to a special class of people, whose souls have reached such a pitch that, assisted by intense conjunction with intelligible principles, they 'become intuitively inflamed', as happens in the case of those individuals who have reached the highest rank of prophethood (*nubuwwah*).[7]

On the question of survival after death, the position of al-Fārābi, as we have seen, tended to be nuanced. The souls of the inhabitants of the virtuous city, according to him, are destined to survive the destruction of their bodies, in some form or other. Those of the inhabitants of the ignorant cities, like those of beasts, will simply perish upon departing the bodies in which they were incarcerated during their terrestrial existence. Ibn Sīna, by contrast, is eloquent, both in his philosophical works and in his famous poem *On the Soul*, in asserting that the soul, as such, is incorruptible and does not cease to exist with the cessation of the body. His chief argument in support of this view is that the relation of the soul to the body is purely accidental, so that the causes of the corruption of the body, which is a compound of material elements and humors, will not affect the soul in the least, being entirely simple and incorruptible.[8] It will return upon leaving the 'wilderness'; of terrestrial existence, like a dove, as Ibn Sīna expresses it in his above-mentioned poem, to its higher abode in the intelligible world. Significantly, however, Ibn Sīna does not rule out bodily resurrection, which was at the center of the controversy between the Neoplatonists and the Mutakallimun. He distinguishes instead between two modes of resurrection: a) that of the soul, which is known through reason and demonstrative proof, and b) that of the body, which is known through religious instruction. This form of resurrection and the pleasures and pains that the body will experience in the life-to-come 'can only be known through the holy law [*sharī'ah*] and assent to prophetic

7. Cf. *al-Najāt*, p. 206.
8. Ibid., pp. 225f.

reports'. For 'The true holy law, which our chosen Prophet Muhammad has brought us, has actually laid down for us the conditions of bodily happiness or misery in the life-to-come'.[9]

That law, Ibn Sīna is categorical, has confirmed spiritual resurrection, which is demonstratively known, as well as bodily resurrection, which rests on the authority of that holy law and cannot therefore be questioned.

Among Ibn Sīna's major contributions to 'natural theology' or metaphysics, which Etienne Gilson has acknowledged and underlined, is the concept of the Necessary Being, as the ultimate principle upon which the whole series of contingent entities in the world depend. In this context, Ibn Sīna is credited with the formulation of one of the major arguments for the existence of God, known as the argument *a contingentia mundi* (Arabic, *dalīl al-jawāz*), which is associated with the name of the German philosopher Leibniz (d. 1714) in modern philosophy, but which St. Thomas Aquinas gave in the *Summa Theologica*, I, Q. 2, as the third 'way' for proving the existence of God, drawing ultimately on Ibn Sīna's Latin translation of *al-Shifā'*, known as *Sufficiencia*.[10]

However, it is to be noted that here, too, Ibn Sīna's debt to al-Fārābi is well-attested. For in one of his shorter tracts, *'Uyūn al-Masā'il* (or *Principal Issues*), al-Fārābi draws a sharp distinction between entities that considered in themselves, are seen to be possible or contingent, and those which considered in themselves are seen to be necessary. A characteristic of the possible, he goes on to argue, is that it can be supposed, without contradiction, not to exist. Accordingly, it cannot dispense for its coming into being with a cause, whereby it becomes necessary through another, a favorite expression of Ibn Sīna. Similarly, al-Fārābi asserts, as Ibn Sīna does in formulating his own proof of the existence of the Necessary Being, that the series of possible entities cannot go on to infinity, either in succession or in a circle. They must instead culminate in a Necessary Being who is the First (*Awwal*), as al-Fārābi prefers to call Him. Such a Being, according to Ibn Sīna, cannot, unlike the possible, be supposed not to exist without self-contradiction.

9. Ibid., p. 326.
10. Cf. Gilson, *Les Sources Gréco-arabes de l'Augustinisme avicennisant*, *Archives d'histoire doctrinale et littéraire du Moyen Age*, 4, 1929, pp. 5–107.

It is in addition uncaused and is perfect, since it is free from all forms of deficiency (*naqṣ*).

Like his successor, al-Fārābi also asserts that the First has no essence or quiddity (*māhiyah*). Its essence consists simply in being the Necessary Being and, as such, the First has no genus or differentia. It is for this reason indefinable and indemonstrable, since it is the demonstration or proof (*burhān*) of all other things. It is, in addition, as we have seen earlier, pure intellect, intelligible and act of intellection (*'aql wa 'āqil wa ma'qūl*), at one and the same time. Moreover, as the Being who possesses the utmost beauty, it is the first lover (*'āshiq*) and the first object of love (*ma'shūq*).[11]

Al-Fārābi does not develop explicitly here or elsewhere the argument from contingency, associated, as we have seen, with the name of Ibn Sīna in the Middle Ages and that of Leibniz in modern times. Notwithstanding, his account of the Necessary Being, as distinct from the possible entities that depend for their existence on Him, clearly shows that he laid the groundwork of that argument, which Ibn Sīna later developed in a systematic way. It is possible, however, as I have argued elsewhere,[12] that al-Fārābi favored the other Augustinian-Platonic argument known as the ontological. That argument is generally associated with the name of the Archbishop of Canterbury, St. Anselm (d. 1109), and that of the famous French philosopher and mathematician René Descartes (d. 1650). In fact, al-Fārābi describes the Supreme Being in his *Fuṣūl* as 'the First Truth which imparts truth to other things ... Indeed, no greater perfection than His perfection can be imagined, let alone exist'[13] – a statement reminiscent of St. Anselm speaking of the Supreme Being as 'nothing greater than whom can be conceived'.[14]

Nevertheless, it is striking that al-Fārābi has nowhere developed this argument at any length either. He appears in fact to regard the existence of the One as intuitively certain and accordingly not requiring any demonstration. In fact, the One or First is for him both indefinable and indemonstrable.[15]

11. *'Uyūn al-Masā'il* (Dieterici), pp. 57f. Cf. *al-Madīnah al-Fāḍilah.*
12. Cf. Fakhry, 'The Ontological Argument in the Arabic Tradition: The Case of al-Fārābi'.
13. *Fuṣūl*, p. 53.
14. Cf. *Proslogion*, III.
15. Cf. *al-Madīnah al-Fāḍilah*, p. 30.

Al-Ghazāli's onslaught on al-Fārābi and Ibn Sīna

Despite the great strides it made in the tenth and eleventh centuries, Neoplatonism was soon the target of attack by Ash'arite theologians, who were generally averse to the study of logic and Greek philosophy in general. The most devastating such attack was that of Abū Hāmid al-Ghazāli (d. 1111), generally regarded as the greatest theologian or Proof of Islam (*Hujjat al-Islām*). He was the disciple of the other great Ash'arite theologian, al-Juwayni (d. 1086), with whom he studied philosophy and logic, two subjects to which he contributed two important treatises, the *Intentions of the Philosophers* (*Maqāsid al-Falāsifah*) and the *Criterion of Knowledge* (*Mi'yār al-'Ilm*), which attest to his thorough knowledge of Greek philosophy and Aristotelian logic.

Al-Ghazāli's attack on Islamic Neoplatonism is embodied in his great polemical treatise, the *Incoherence of the Philosophers* (*Tahāfūt al-Falāsifah*). In the preface, he states that his aim is to show 'the contradiction inherent in the opinions of their leader, the Absolute Philosopher and First Teacher [i.e. Aristotle] best rendered and interpreted by al-Fārābi and Ibn Sīna, his best two expositors among the *philosophizers* of Islam'.[16] He proceeds to list and discuss twenty propositions or 'questions' which are either fully or in part 'in conflict with the fundamentals of religion [i.e. Islam]'.[17] Of these questions, three are singled out by him as particularly pernicious from a religious (Islamic) point of view: the eternity of the world, the denial of God's knowledge of particulars and the denial of the resurrection of the body. On these three questions, the Muslim philosophers, with al-Fārābi and Ibn Sīna at their head, should be declared infidels (*takfīr*), according to him. On the remaining seventeen propositions, those philosophers should be declared heretics or innovators (*tabdī'*) only.

These less pernicious questions, in the opinion of al-Ghazāli, include the post-eternity of the world (*abadiyah*), a corollary of pre-eternity (*qidam*) and the inability of the philosophers to prove the existence of God, as Creator of the world, since they believed it to be eternal and

16. *Tahāfūt al-Falāsifah*, p. 9.
17. Ibid., p. 13.

therefore requiring no creator. Thus, when the philosophers speak of God as Creator of the world, al-Ghazāli charges, they are simply engaged in dissimulation or double-talk (*talbīs*).

Equally pernicious and gratuitous, al-Ghazāli goes on to argue, is the whole emanationist scheme, which, as we have seen, formed the cornerstone of the metaphysics and cosmology of al-Fārābi and other Muslim Neoplatonists. This scheme rests on the arbitrary premise that out of the One only one can come, which they then proceed to interpret in a variety of preposterous ways, which, 'were one to refer to a dream he saw in his sleep, he would be thought to suffer from a foul humor'.[18] The philosophers then go on to show, al-Ghazāli adds, that the One has no knowledge of the world He has created, robbing Him thereby of the attributes of life, knowledge and will and reducing Him to the status of the dead.[19]

An equally devastating attack is launched against the philosophers' thesis that the correlation between causes and effects is necessary and irreversible. For al-Ghazāli, neither reason nor observation confirms this thesis, which is rooted in the habitual observation of that correlation, which is far from being necessary. God, as the Sole Agent in the universe, can always bring about its suspension, as happens in miracles, with the possibility of which all Muslims concur.[20]

Ibn Bājjah and the Andalusian interlude

The impact of al-Ghazāli's attack on philosophy was historically profound and long-lasting. In the circles of the Mutakallimun, especially the Ash'arites, the downfall of philosophy was almost complete, especially in the eastern parts of the Islamic empire. Al-Ghazāli's onslaught is explicitly leveled at al-Fārābi and Ibn Sīna, the two champions of Neoplatonism in Islam. The former was, as we have seen, the founder of that late brand of Hellenic philosophy, initiated in the Hellenistic world by Plotinus and Proclus, the latter its chief expositor. The twenty

18. *Tahāfūt al-Tahāfūt*, p. 116.
19. Ibid., pp. 120 and 131.
20. Ibid., p. 276.

'questions' that formed the core of al-Ghazāli's onslaught were at the center of the controversy that pitted the Mutakallimun against the philosophers of Islam. This controversy had started, in fact, well before al-Ghazāli's publication of his *Incoherence of the Philosophers* (*Tahāfūt al-Falāsifah*) in 1085. It is significant, however, that it did not completely silence the philosophers, Neoplatonists or others, as the rebuttals of al-Ghazāli's arguments by some of his successors, especially Ibn Rushd of Cordova (d. 1198), better known as Averroes, show.

However, philosophy was destined to gain a new lease of life in Muslim Spain (*al-Andalus*), at the hands of a number of philosophers, including Ibn Bājjah (d. 1138), Ibn Tufay (d. 1186) and Ibn Rushd.

Abū Bakr Ibn al-Sāyiqh, also known as Ibn Bājjah, was the first noteworthy philosopher of *al-Andalus*, and is credited with a series of commentaries or glosses on a large number of Aristotelian works, including the *Physics*, *On Generation and Corruption*, the *Zoological Treatises*, *De Anima* and *Meteorologica*.

Of his Eastern masters, almost the only philosopher he refers to constantly, and the one he appears to regard as his mentor in politics, ethics and logic, is al-Fārābi, with whose works he was thoroughly conversant. Of these works, Ibn Bājjah mentions al-Fārābi's lost commentary on the *Nicomachean Ethics*, known in Arabic sources as *Niqumachia*, and his treatise *On Unity*, as well as the whole logical corpus, with the exception of *Rhetorica* and *Poetica*. Among Ibn Bājjah's major logical writings is a series of extensive glosses (*ta'āliq*) on al-Fārābi's logical treatises, including the *Categories*, the *Five Sections*, *On Interpretation* (*Kitāb al-'Ibarah*), *Analytica Priora* (*Kitāb al-Qiyās*) and *Analytica Posteriora* (*Kitāb al-Burhān*).[21]

More substantively, Ibn Bājjah's political philosophy and ethics are thoroughly al-Fārābian in content. Thus, in his major political treatise, the *Conduct of the Solitary* (*Tadbīr al-Mutawaḥḥid*), he portrays the 'solitary', or genuine philosopher, as one who seeks conjunction (*ittiṣāl*) with the Active Intellect, fulfilling thereby his highest intellectual aspiration, as al-Fārābi did. However, such a philosopher is confronted with a serious

21. See Ibn Bājjah, *Ta'āliq Ibn Bājjah 'ala Mantiq al-Fārābi*.

obstacle; his aspirations can only be fulfilled in a 'perfect' or virtuous city. Such a city, however, may be non-existent, and thus the plight of such a solitary might become desperate. In these circumstances, as al-Fārābi also argued, such a seeker of knowledge and virtue will have no choice but to 'keep away from his fellowmen as far as possible; consort with them only in necessary matters or emigrate to cities in which the sciences flourish, if such [cities] existed',[22] as Ibn Bājjah writes.

Like al-Fārābi, Ibn Bājjah dwells on the degeneration of the perfect (virtuous) city into timocracy, democracy and tyranny. The perfect city, as Plato argued in the *Republic*, is one that is in no need of physicians or judges. For its inhabitants are held together by the bond of love. Accordingly, there is no strife between them, and therefore they have no use for judges. Moreover, since those inhabitants are addicted to gymnastics and feed on healthy foods, their bodies are not liable to sickness and, in the event of sickness, are able to heal spontaneously. Hence, they have no use for physicians either.[23]

With respect to actions and opinions, Ibn Bājjah argues next that it is characteristic of the perfect city that all the actions of its inhabitants are right and their opinions are true. Should wrong actions or false opinions be found in that city, that should be attributed to the class of outgrowths (*nawābit*), of which al-Fārābi spoke in his *Civil Polity* (*al-Siyāsah al-Madaniyah*). However, Ibn Bājjah diverges from his master, who appears to confine the existence of that aberrant class to the virtuous city, as he explicitly states.[24]

For Ibn Bājjah, by contrast, it is characteristic of the perfect or virtuous city that there are no outgrowths in it. In fact, Ibn Bājjah appears to imply that that term applies exclusively to those who 'subscribe to opinion(s) other than those of the inhabitants of the city, whether true or false';[25] by whom he obviously meant the inhabitants of the degenerate city. For it is characteristic of the perfect or virtuous city, as he asserts, that there are no false opinions or wrong actions in it. By contrast, outgrowths, physicians

22. *Tadbīr al-Mutawaḥḥid*, in Ibn Bājjah, *Opera Metaphysica*, p. 90. Cf. al-Fārābi, *Fuṣūl*, p. 65.
23. Cf. Ibid., p. 41. Cf. *Republic*, III, 405 *c*.
24. Cf. *al-Siyāsah al-Madaniyah*, pp. 86 and 104.
25. *Tadbīr al-Mutawaḥḥid*, p. 41.

and judges abound in the degenerate cities, including 'all those regimes which exist in our own time and in most preceding times, as we have been informed'. He excludes, on the authority of al-Fārābi, the 'original regimes of the Persians'.[26]

Nevertheless, the class of outgrowths can contribute to the reformation of the degenerate regimes in which they live, insofar as some of them may light on a 'true opinion' that did not previously exist in that city; the more such opinions are lighted upon by the outgrowths the better. For that reason, the existence of outgrowths in the four degenerate forms of government, already mentioned, may be said to be the 'cause of the rise of the perfect city',[27] as he puts it. This is a role that al-Fārābi, in his account of that aberrant class, which arises within the virtuous state, does not envisage.

In ethics, Ibn Bājjah is committed to the same moral and eschatological ideals as al-Fārābi. The ultimate goal of human endeavor for him cannot be pleasure, whether sensuous or intellectual. Even the alleged spiritual pleasures, which Sufis, such as al-Ghazāli, commend or claim to have experienced, cannot be equated with that ultimate goal;[28] nor is it honor, wealth or piety. That goal for him, as it was for al-Fārābi, is 'theoretical knowledge' (*'ilm naẓari*), with which humankind's highest perfection is bound up. That perfection corresponds, as al-Fārābi also held, with that stage of cognition called the acquired intellect, which humans attain upon 'conjunction' with the Active Intellect. At this point, the intellect and its object (*ma'qūl*) are thoroughly identified, since the intellect is then free of multiplicity and involves no mode of composition such as that of matter and form. 'Speculation [*naẓar*] in that sense', Ibn Bājjah writes, 'is equivalent to life in the world-to-come and constitutes the ultimate, solitary human felicity [*sa'ādah*].'[29] Al-Fārābi, it will be recalled, did not confine that felicity or happiness to this otherworldly variety, but appears to have regarded it as possible in this world, as well, when the two conditions of virtue and knowledge have been fulfilled.

26. Ibid., p. 43.
27. Ibid.
28. Ibid., p. 121.
29. Ibid., p. 166.

Ibn Rushd (Averroes)

The great Andalusian philosopher, Averroes (d. 1198), who rehabilitated Aristotle following al-Ghazāli's devastating onslaught, was highly critical of the Neoplatonic scheme developed by al-Fārābi and Ibn Sīna. His major strictures bear on the viability of the emanationist scheme, which he says is 'something about which the [ancient] company [*qawm*] [by whom he meant Aristotle and his followers] knew nothing',[30] implying that the responsibility for popularizing it in Arabic should be imputed to al-Fārābi and Ibn Sīna.

The chief objection to this scheme, according to Averroes, is that its exponents have reduced the Invisible Agent (or God) to the same status as the visible agent, human or natural. Having observed that the visible agent operates in a uniform manner, they concluded that God can only operate in a uniform manner, which they expressed in their famous maxim that out of the one, only one can come. According to them, especially al-Fārābi, who was the first to introduce the whole emanationist scheme in Arabic, the First Being or the One, generates the first intellect, who generates the second intellect and the corresponding heavenly spheres, until we reach the tenth intellect which governs the sublunary world. This view, argues Averroes, amounts to a serious derogation from the perfection of God, who is able to operate in any way He pleases.[31]

Another major criticism leveled at both al-Fārābi and Ibn Sīna is that their distinction between the possible and the necessary, which they use as the basis of their argument for the existence of God or the Necessary Being, as they call Him, is faulted logically. To prove the existence of the Necessary Being, as we have seen, they argue that the world, being possible in itself can only come into being through another who is necessary, to whom they refer, for that reason, as the Necessary Being. It follows that the world is possible in itself, but necessary through another, which amounts to 'converting the nature of the possible into that of the necessary', which is logically absurd, according to Averroes.[32] In fact, the

30. *Tahāfūt al-Tahāfūt*, p. 182.
31. Ibid., pp. 179f.
32. *Tafsīr mā Ba'd al-Tabi'ah*, III, p. 1632.

Arabic sources attribute to Averroes a polemical tract aimed at Ibn Sīna, but applying by extension to al-Fārābi, entitled 'Refutation of Ibn Sīna's division of existing entities into what is possible absolutely, what is possible in itself but necessary through another and what is necessary in itself'.

Moreover, Averroes goes on to argue, the thesis that the world is possible or contingent, as they claim, is untenable. For once we posit the series of causes, whether natural or heavenly, which determine the sequence of events in the lower world, everything in that world ceases to be possible and becomes necessary, by reason of the necessity of the causal nexus that holds existing entities together. Thus, whoever repudiates the necessity pertaining to this nexus is forced to repudiate the wisdom of the Maker and to refer everything in the world to chance or random (*ittifāq*).[33] In fact, Averroes goes one step further in his critique, arguing that the recognition of the necessary causal nexus is synonymous with the recognition of the authority of reason; so that 'whoever repudiates causes actually repudiates reason'.[34]

It is not surprising in the circumstances that Averroes, in his response to al-Ghazāli in the *Tahāfūt*, should dissociate himself somewhat from both al-Fārābi and Ibn Sīna. He often accuses those two Neoplatonists of having either distorted or misunderstood the intent of Aristotle. As for al-Ghazāli, their arch-critic, he is often accused either of dogmatism or downright sophistry.

Thus, in his rebuttal of al-Ghazāli's first major attack on the philosophers for adhering to the proposition that the world is eternal, Averroes challenges that theologian to produce a single Qur'anic verse that asserts unequivocally the contrary thesis that the world is created out of nothing and in time (*muḥdath*). To the contrary, Averroes argues, those verses, such as Qur'an 11:6, which states, 'It is He who created the heavens and the earth in six days, and His throne was upon the water', imply on the surface of it that the creation of the world was preceded by the Throne, the water and the time that measures their duration. Similarly, Qur'an 41:10, which states, 'Then He arose to heaven while it was smoke',

33. *Al-Kashf*, pp. 145 and 200.
34. *Tahāfūt*, p. 412.

implies that the world was actually created from a pre-existing matter, which was smoke. Finally, of the two modes of creation or origination of the world, continuous (*dā'im*) and discontinuous (*munqati'*), it is obvious that the former is more appropriately attributed to God, who could not have been barred from creating the world throughout eternity by any external impediment or deficiency on His part.[35]

On the second major criticism or the philosophers' alleged denial of God's knowledge of particulars, Averroes argues that the fallacy of Ibn Sīna's thesis that God knows everything created, by a universal mode of knowledge, which al-Ghazāli rejects, consists in the false analogy between divine and human knowledge upon which the whole controversy turns. For Averroes, God's knowledge cannot be described either as universal or as particular, for its modality, like that of His will, is unknown to us.[36] It is, in other words, a mode of knowledge *sui generis.*

On the third major criticism, that the philosophers deny the resurrection of the body, Averroes reveals his greatest subtlety. To begin with, the philosophers do not question the *fact* of survival after death (*ma'ād*), but only its *mode*, which raises the acutest questions. For, rationally considered, such survival is found to entail a series of absurdities. It is supposed, in fact, by the advocates of bodily resurrection that, upon being brought back to life on the Day of Judgment, the same soul is reunified to the same body which dissolved upon death, into dust, which was absorbed by a vegetable, which was in turn consumed by a human male and then transformed into a sperm, which finally gave rise to another human, male or female.

This supposition, argues Averroes, is clearly absurd. Notwithstanding, the philosophers do not question the reunion of the soul and body upon resurrection; but rather the fact that it is rationally demonstrable. Such resurrection, according to them, is religiously affirmed as unquestionable. For all religious laws (*sharā'i'*), he observes, concur in asserting the resurrection, although they differ in their account of the misery or bliss reserved for the soul in the after-life. 'It is likely', he writes, 'that the representation [of misery and bliss] found in our religion [i.e. Islam] is more

35. *Tahāfut*, pp. 95f. and 162.
36. Ibid., p. 149.

conducive to instructing most people and more affective in inciting their souls to seek that bliss';[37] 'spiritual representations' being less effective where the majority of people are concerned. The philosophers therefore do not deny 'bodily resurrection', 'on which none of the ancients had anything to say'.[38] The reason Averroes gives is essentially historical: this doctrine, according to him, goes back no further than a thousand years, and is attributed to the prophets of Israel, who antedate the philosophers known to us,[39] and had no knowledge of it. However, such a religious doctrine serves a profound moral and political purpose and for that reason should not be questioned. Averroes reiterates in this context his grand thesis that the difference between philosophy and religion is reducible in the last analysis to the fact that 'philosophy seeks to determine the intellectual felicity of some people', unlike religion, which aims at instructing the general public.[40] He is categorical that the soul is immortal, as attested by both philosophy and religion, but the bodies to which souls are reunited upon resurrection, according to him, are *analogous* to, rather than identical with, the bodies from which they were separated at death.[41]

In the field of logic, to which the contributions of both al-Fārābi and Averroes were very significant, the latter, who was definitely influenced by the former, is nevertheless critical of him on the general ground that his 'viewpoint was at variance with that of Aristotle', as a lost treatise of Averroes expressed it. In another lost treatise, Averroes criticizes al-Fārābi for 'diverging from Aristotle in his *Book of Demonstration* (*Kitāb al-Burhān*) with respect to the arrangement [of topics dealt with] and the canons of proof and definition'.

Despite these and similar methodological criticisms, there is no question that Averroes was influenced by the method of commentary and paraphrase which al-Fārābi applied to parts of the Aristotelian logical corpus, as we saw in Chapter 1. The list of al-Fārābi's logical writings includes a series of large commentaries, of which the commentary on the *Perhermenias* (*Kitāb*

37. *Al-Kashf*, p. 244.
38. *Tahāfūt*, p. 580.
39. Ibid., p. 580. Averroes refers to 'those from whom we received philosophy', by whom he probably meant the translators of the eighth and ninth centuries.
40. Ibid., p. 582.
41. Ibid., p. 586. Cf. *al-Kashf*, pp. 245f.

al-'Ibārah) has survived. This, as everybody knows, became Averroes' characteristic method of commenting not only on Aristotle's logical works, but on the whole of his major writings, including the *Physics*, the *Metaphysics*, *De Anima* and the *Nicomachean Ethics*, which have all survived either in Arabic or in Latin translations. Al-Fārābi also wrote a series of paraphrases and summaries of a large number of logical treatises, which correspond to a parallel series of Averroist paraphrases and summaries.

Averroes is nevertheless critical of al-Fārābi on a variety of specific logical points. Thus, in his *Summary of the Categories*, he criticizes al-Fārābi's view of the relation of the accident to the definition, based on his distinction between the universal accident, such as whiteness, and the particular accident, such as white. This relation Aristotle denied, asserting that the definition of the color white (i.e. whiteness) is never predicable of the subject.[42]

With respect to possible premises, Averroes disagrees with al-Fārābi's claim that when the possible and the necessary premises are conjoined, the conclusion is universal, contrary to Aristotle's view, which, according to Averroes, is obvious by induction. For when the major premise is necessary and the minor is possible, the syllogism is incomplete and the conclusion is far from being universal. Where the major premise is possible and the minor is necessary, the opposite is true. Averroes gives as an example the following instance: 'Every man *may* walk', which is true of all men, potentially and actually; whereas 'All men *must* walk' is not, since cripples cannot walk.[43]

Averroes also criticizes al-Fārābi's argument that a conditional syllogism can yield a necessary conclusion, insofar as necessity is part of the second or minor premise. This claim is rejected by Averroes on the ground that necessity is not an essential feature of the syllogism or any part thereof, but rather an accidental or subsidiary one. Thus, if we say, for instance, 'If the sun is up, it is day', we would be justified in inferring by induction from the statement 'it is day' that the sun is up; or from 'it is not day' that the sun is not up. The same is true of disjunction; thus, we are justified in saying, 'It is not day, therefore, it is night.' According to

42. Cf. *Talkhīs al-Maqūlāt*, p. 88 and Aristotle, *Categories*, 1 *b* 30.
43. *Talkhīs k. al-Qiyās*, p. 132.

Averroes, the view of Aristotle is that the conclusion in all these syllogisms is possible by induction, since from the particular case 'it is day' or 'the sun is up' no universal or necessary conclusion can be drawn.[44] In fact, those instances belong to the category of 'propositional logic', which the Stoics developed and to which Aristotle did not accord sufficient attention.

In the discussion of rhetoric, Averroes tends to agree with al-Fārābi on a variety of points. To begin with, they both regarded rhetoric as part of logic, insofar as it aims, like dialectic (*jadal*), at persuasion (*iqnā'*). Al-Fārābi, however, added an historical note to this argument, since for him, as we saw earlier, rhetoric preceded dialectic in time and the two continued to be used, together with sophistry, until Plato's time. Those methods of persuasion were eventually superseded by demonstration, whose rules were codified by Aristotle.[45]

Secondly, after referring to al-Fārābi's discussion of the four forms of government – namely, democracy, oligarchy, aristocracy and monarchy – mentioned by Aristotle in *Rhetorica*, I, 1365 *b*, Averroes comments that the rhetorician should use the kinds of logical arguments which are more effective in persuading the audience, as Aristotle puts it. He adds, however, a more specific condition; namely, that the rhetorician should 'master the language of the people he is addressing', and place the 'terms of conjunction [*rawābīt*]' in their proper places; adding that these *terms* of conjunction are given by al-Fārābi in many of his writings, including in particular al-Fārābi's treatise entitled the *Terms Used in Logic*. Averroes then endorses al-Fārābi's statement, probably in his large commentary on *Rhetorica*, which has not survived, that eloquence (*balāqhah*) for Arab orators consisted in the use of straightforward speech (*qawl ghayr marbūt*), by which he probably meant open-ended disquisition (*istitrād*), which was actually a feature of Arab oratory from the earliest times. Such eloquence depended likewise, as stated by al-Fārābi, on avoiding the use of synonyms, negations and indefinite terms, except in satire (*hijā'*) or allusion (*tawriyah*).[46]

44. Ibid., p. 195.
45. *Kitāb al-Hurūf*, p. 132.
46. Cf. Ibn Rushd, *Talkhīs al-Khatabah*, pp. 272f.

Thirdly, with respect to poetry, Averroes and al-Fārābi were in agreement that, as al-Fārābi puts it, 'The essence or aim of poetry, according to the ancients [i.e. Aristotle and his followers] was a form of composite speech simulating the object in question',[47] adding that such simulation (*muhākāt, mimesis*) could take the form of a statement or an action aiming at representing that object imaginatively. From this, al-Fārābi then inferred that poetic imagination is analogous to knowledge in demonstration, conjecture in dialectic and persuasion in rhetoric, and accordingly forms part of the 'syllogistic arts'. This is what justifies for al-Fārābi the inclusion of poetics in the logical corpus. Averroes appears to agree with this view, arguing in his *Talkhīs Kitāb al-Shi'r* (*Summary of the Poetics*) 'that the imaginative arts or those which function like imagination are three: rhyme, meter and the use of simulated discourse',[48] which he identifies with the function of poetry, too. Neither al-Fārābi nor Averroes appears to have been aware of the fact that this view of poetry was diametrically opposed to that of Aristotle, who held that 'the poet's function is to describe, not the thing that has happened, but a kind of thing, that might happen, i.e. what is possible, as being probable or necessary'.[49] It follows that the study of poetry lies outside the scope of logic, which is exclusively concerned with the actual, insofar as it is susceptible of truth or falsity.

Neoplatonism and Sufism

A further instance of the resilience of Neoplatonism is that despite the devastating onslaught of al-Ghazāli, and the Ash'arites in general, it continued to make strides in Sufi circles. Perhaps the most significant such strides are those associated with the way in which the Ishrāqi philosophers, led by Shihāb al-Dīn al-Suhrawardi (d. 1191), succeeded in reconciling it with mysticism. In his *al-Tabwīhāt* (*Allusions*), al-Suhrawardi accuses the Peripatetics of his day (by whom he meant the Neoplatonists, or the followers of al-Fārābi and Ibn Sīna) of having misunderstood the

47. *Jawāni' al-Shi'r*, appendix to Ibn Rushd, *Talkhīs Kitāb Aristutālis fi'l-Shi'r* of Averroes, p. 172.
48. *Talkhīs K. al-Shi'r*, p. 58.
49. Aristotle, *Poetics*, IX, 1451 *a* 35.

teaching of Aristotle (by whom he meant Plotinus). This Aristotle, we are told in *Hikmat al-Ishrāq* (*Wisdom of Illumination*), appeared to him in a dream and assured him of the unity of the discursive (*baḥthiyah*) and the experiential (*dhawqiyah*), of philosophy and mysticism, embodied in the philosophies of Plato, Hermes and Pythagoras, and, beyond them, in the teachings of the Persian sages of antiquity, Jamasp, Framashaustra, Bizirgimhr, Zoroaster and their predecessors in the East.[50] In this 'philosophy of illumination' (*Ishrāq*), traces of which are already discernible in Ibn Sīna's later writings, especially the *Allusions and Indications* (*al-Ishārāt wa'l-Tanbīhāt*) and the *Short Mystical Treatises*,[51] Neoplatonism and Sufism are reconciled for the first time in the history of Islamic thought. The emanationist scheme is accepted with some qualifications and the hierarchy of intellects is replaced by a hierarchy of lights, at the top of which stands the Light of Lights (*Nūr al-Anwār*), corresponding to al-Fārābi's First Principle (*al-Awwal*) and Ibn Sīna's Necessary Being. From the Light of Lights, according to al-Suhrawardi, emanates the series of subordinate lights, beginning with the first light, which corresponds to al-Fārābi's first intellect, followed by the secondary lights, the heavenly bodies and finally the world of the elements.

In another respect, al-Suhrawardi appears to be convinced, like al-Fārābi and Ibn Sīna, of the eternity of the world as an emanation from the Light of Lights. This world, according to him, arises by way of combination or admixture of contrary qualities or natures, culminating in the emergence of the 'human light', or rational soul. This soul is fated, upon its liberation from the 'terrestrial lights' or material elements and compounds, to be released from the bondage of the body and to rejoin its original abode in the world of lights, where it will be united to the 'holy spirits' dwelling in the world of pure light, corresponding to al-Fārābi's intelligible world.[52]

The Ishrāqi philosophy reached its zenith in the works of Sadr al-Dīn al-Shīrāzi (d. 1641) and has dominated Persian Shi'ite thought ever since.

50. *Hikmat al-Ishrāq*, p. 10. Cf. *al-Mashāri'*, pp. 483f. and *Talwīhāt*, pp. 38f., in al-Suhrawardi, *Oeuvres philosophiques et mystiques*.
51. Cf. Fakhry, *A History of Islamic Philosophy*, pp. 157f.
52. Cf. *Ḥikmat al-Ishrāq*, p. 252.

Al-Shīrāzi was influenced by Ibn Sīna's Neoplatonic thought, on the one hand, and Ibn 'Arabi's mystical thought, on the other. Like that great Sufi of *al-Andalus*, who died in 1240, al-Shīrāzi speaks of 'the possible entities', corresponding to Ibn 'Arabi's 'fixed essences', as the primary manifestations of the Supreme Reality (corresponding to the intelligible forms of the Neoplatonists). Those possible essences are then identified with the Supreme Reality (*al-Ḥaqq*) itself, which is in turn identified with the creation (*khalq*), as Ibn 'Arabi also maintained. In this way, the unity of all beings, the Creator and the creature, the spiritual and the material worlds, is assured, as both philosophy and mysticism actually teach, according to al-Shīrāzi.

Al-Fārābi and the West

In the western part of Muslim Spain (*al-Andalus*), perhaps the most lavish tribute paid al-Fārābi was that of the great Jewish Aristotelian, Moses Maimonides (d. 1204). In a letter addressed to his disciple Samuel Ben Tibbon, Maimonides writes, 'The works of Aristotle are the roots and foundations of works on the sciences, and cannot be understood except with the help of commentaries, those of Alexander of Aphrodisias, those of Themistius and those of Averroes. I tell you, as for works on logic, one should only study the writings of Abū Naṣr al-Fārābi. All his works are faultlessly excellent. One ought to study and understand them; for he was a great man.'[53]

Moreover, Maimonides refers in his *Guide of the Perplexed* to al-Fārābi's books, including his *Epistle on the Intellect*, his book *On Changing Entities*, and the *Commentary on the Nicomachean Ethics*. The last two books are no longer extant, hence the importance of those references. In the case of both the *Epistle on the Intellect* and the *Glosses on the Physics*, Maimonides quotes the words of al-Fārābi verbatim in the course of discussing his views.

As for the Latin West, it is fairly well-known that by the end of the twelfth century a large number of Arabic medical, scientific and philosophical works had been translated into Latin, sometimes via the Hebrew medium or with the assistance of Jewish scholars. The most famous

53. Cf. Maimonides, 'Letter to Samuel Ben Tibbon', pp. 552–3.

and prolific translator of that period was Gerard of Cremona (d. 1187), who is credited with no fewer than eighty treatises translated from Arabic. Other translators included Dominicus Gundissalinus (Gundisalvi), Avendanth, also known as John of Seville, and Herman of Carinthia. This first group of translators from Arabic was followed in the next century by others, such as Herman the German (Hermannuus Alemannus) (d. 1272), Michael the Scot (d. 1236), Mark of Toledo and others.

Of al-Fārābi's works, the earliest Latin translation was the *Enumeration of the Sciences* (*Iḥṣā' al-'Ulūm*), first translated by Gundissalinus around 1140 and later by Gerard of Cremona under the title *Liber Alfarabii de Scientiis*.[54] This was followed by the *Epistle on the Intellect*, translated by Gundissalinus into Latin, too, and more recently into French by Etienne Gilson.[55]

Particularly noteworthy is the Latin translation of al-Fārābi's *Commentary on the Nicomachean Ethics*, mentioned in the Arabic sources, but no longer extant in Arabic. References to this work, accompanied sometimes by quotations from it, occur in the writings of Albert the Great (d. 1284), teacher of St. Thomas Aquinas (d. 1274),[56] and, as mentioned earlier, Maimonides. A less important compendium of Aristotle's *Rhetorica* is attributed to Hermannus Alemannus and is extant in several Renaissance editions dating back to 1256.[57] This is followed by al-Fārābi's commentary on Aristotle's *Physics*, mentioned in the Arabic sources, but no longer extant in Arabic either. The Latin translation is referred to or quoted by Roger Bacon (d. 1294), Albert the Great and others.[58]

Of al-Fārābi's logical works, a commentary on *Analytica Posteriora* (*Kitāb al-Burhān*) is referred to and quoted by Albert the Great also. This commentary is probably different from the shorter paraphrase I published in 1987.[59] Other Latin authors, including Aegidius Romanus and Peter of St. Amour, quote the *Logica* of al-Fārābi, which is probably different from the large commentary on *Analytica Posteriora* mentioned above.

54. Edited and published by A.G. Palencia, Madrid, 1932.
55. Cf. Bédoret, 'Les premières traductions Tolédanes de philosophy; Oeuvres d'Al-Farabi', p. 84; and 'Les sources gréco-arabes de l'Augustinisme avicennisant', *Archives d'histoire doctrinale et littéraire du moyen âge, Appendix*, IV, 1929, pp. 108–41.
56. Cf. Salmon, 'The Medieval Latin Translations of Alfarabi's Works', p. 247.
57. Ibid., p. 246.
58. Ibid., p. 255.
59. See Bibliography.

Compared with the vast output of al-Fārābi in Arabic, these Latin translations constitute a meager legacy, especially if set against the much longer legacy of Ibn Sīna and Averroes in Latin. However, they are enough to illustrate al-Fārābi's impact on Latin scholars of the thirteenth century, the golden age of Latin Scholasticism.

Conclusion

This study has shown, it is hoped, the standing of al-Fārābi as a major link in the transmission of Greek philosophy to the Arab and Muslim worlds. His erudition was vast, as his extensive references to and comments on the Greek philosophers, especially Plato and Aristotle and even the Presocratic philosophers, clearly show. In his attempt to reconcile Plato and Aristotle, he was obviously inspired by the late Hellenistic tradition, of which Porphyry of Tyre (d. 304) was a major representative. That famous disciple and biographer of Plotinus (d. 270), the founder of Neoplatonism, whom al-Fārābi was responsible for introducing into the Muslim world for the first time, is known from Byzantine sources to have written a treatise entitled *That the Opinions of Plato and Aristotle Are the Same* (*Peri tou mian einai ten Platonous kai Aristotelous hairesin*). This title is reminiscent of the title of al-Fārābi's own treatise *The Reconciliation of the Two Sages, Plato, the Divine and Aristotle, the First Master* (*Al-Jam' baina Ra'yay al-Hakīmayn*). In this and other works, al-Fārābi often refers to or quotes the *Uthulūgia*, a spurious compilation of Plotinus's *Enneads* IV, V and VI, wrongly attributed to Aristotle. This *Ūthulūgia* or *Book of Divinity*, as al-Fārābi sometimes calls it, is known today to have been translated by 'Abd al-Masīḥ Ibn Nā'imah al-Ḥimṣi (d. 835). It circulated in learned circles freely and was regarded as a genuine work of Aristotle, on which al-Kindi and Ibn Sīna are known to have written commentaries.

Al-Fārābi never questioned the claim that the *Uthulūgia* was a genuine work of Aristotle – a circumstance that enabled him to attempt the reconciliation of the Two Sages, Plato and Aristotle. It also enabled him to develop a peculiar Neoplatonic scheme, which he believed to be reconcilable with Aristotelianism. In particular, the One of Plotinus, who was above being and thought, is identified with Aristotle's Unmoved Mover, who is the actuality of thought thinking itself, or, as al-Fārābi puts it, the act, subject and object of thought (*'aql wa 'āqil wa ma'qūl*). He believed, no doubt, too, that this scheme was reconcilable with the Islamic system of beliefs, by reason of the exalted position it accorded the One or First, the destiny of the soul after death and especially its account of the origination of the world from the One. The analogy of this origination to the Qur'anic notion of creation *ex nihilo* and in time was later seriously questioned by Ash'arite theologians and others, but had the merit of being the first serious attempt to explain the origination of the world in coherent philosophical terms in the Muslim world.

The influence of Plato on al-Fārābi's thought is almost exclusively limited to his adoption of a utopian political model, in which the perfect state is made to correspond to the Islamic (Shi'ite) polity, in which the philosopher-king is identified with the Imām, and to some extent the Prophet. In addition to Plato's qualifications, the first ruler (*ra'īs*) possesses the Islamic qualifications of eloquence and soundness of bodily organs, which the jurists traditionally ascribed to the caliph.

The perfect state, which al-Fārābi calls the virtuous city (*al-Madīnah al-Fāḍilah*), is represented as the one in which humans are able to achieve the double goal of knowledge and happiness to the highest degree. He does not dwell, as Plato does, on its three principal parts or the way in which they correspond to the three parts of the soul – the rational, the spirited and the appetitive – as given in the *Republic*. And although he discusses the concept of justice in a variety of contexts, he does not lay enough stress on that virtue as the equilibrium or harmony of the three parts of the soul as well as those of the state, as Plato again does.

Al-Fārābi's concept of the relation between the perfect state and inferior forms differs from Plato in one major respect. For Plato, the perfect state devolves progressively into degenerate forms, under the pressure of genetic and psychological factors; whereas al-Fārābi simply refers to those degenerate forms as 'opposites' of the perfect or virtuous state in a somewhat static manner. However, he agrees with Plato, on the whole, on the number of the degenerate forms and how it is possible for other forms (in fact, all the other forms) to grow out of democracy, as Plato also held. Nowhere does al-Fārābi, perhaps out of a sense of Shi'ite caution (*taqiyah*), refer to existing forms of government in his day. He does, however, make the melancholy reflections in his *Political Excerpts* (*Fuṣūl al-Madani*) on the plight of the virtuous person, who should be prohibited from dwelling in corrupt cities, and ought instead to emigrate to any virtuous city, should such a city actually exist in that person's time. If, however, none exists, 'the virtuous man is an unhappy stranger in the world and death is better for him than life'.[1]

For these reasons, it is fair to conclude that the utopian model he calls the 'virtuous city' remains for al-Fārābi far removed from the political realities of his day and is essentially a speculative exercise in the search for the philosophical mode of life suited for a life of contemplation, akin to that of the 'solitary' or mystic. However, like his disciple Ibn Bājjah, al-Fārābi was not well-disposed towards mysticism, especially the practical mysticism of contemporary Sufis, like al-Bistami (d. 887), al-Hallāj (d. 922) or their predecessors.

In ethics, al-Fārābi tended to follow the lead of Aristotle, who regarded *endaimonia*, happiness or felicity (*sa'ādah*), as humankind's ultimate goal, identified by al-Fārābi with the contemplative life. He argues, just as Aristotle does in the *Nicomachean Ethics*, X, 1178 *a* 8, that the essence of humankind, 'more than anything else', is reason, but adds, in a distinct departure from Aristotle in the direction of Neoplatonism, that this essence is thoroughly fulfilled by achieving conjunction (*ittiṣāl*) or, as he sometimes calls it, proximity (*muqārabah*) to the Active Intellect, the tenth emanation from the One and the supermundane agency that governs the sublunary world. The origin of this concept of conjunction which Ibn Sīna fully developed, as indeed of the whole scheme of ten intellects emanating from the One, is not known. Al-Fārābi should be

1. *Fuṣūl*, p. 95.

given credit for introducing it into the Muslim world, influenced perhaps by late Neoplatonic interpreters such as Porphyry, Proclus and Jamblichus.

In the field of logic, al-Fārābi's standing was unmatched. He was the first logician to break with the Syriac (Jacobite-Nestorian) tradition, which flourished at Antioch, Edessa and Qinnesrin, and refused for religious reasons to proceed beyond the first four parts of the Aristotelian logical corpus, i.e. the *Categories*, *Peri hermeneias*, the first part of *Analytica Priora* and the *Isagoge* or *Introduction to the Categories*, written by Porphyry of Tyre. His logical output covered the whole *Organon*, together with the *Rhetorica* and *Poetica*, as well as the *Isagoge* of Porphyry, in the form of paraphrases or large commentaries.

From a historical point of view, it is noteworthy that al-Fārābi was the only outstanding logician during the period separating Boethius (d. 525) and Abélard (d. 1141). William and Martha Kneale, for instance, in their authoritative *Development of Logic*, do not give a single significant logician's name during that period of six hundred years.[2] For this reason, it has been assumed by historians of medieval philosophy and logic that philosophical learning, including Aristotelian logic, completely disappeared following the death of Boethius, who translated into Latin and commented on the whole logical corpus, known as the *Organon*. Today, this assumption should be revised, since the continuity of Aristotelian logic was assured, to a limited extent, from the seventh century on by Syriac-speaking logicians, such as Jacob of Edessa (d. 708), Severus Sebokht (d. 667) and others. From the eighth century on, the logical tradition was continued and expanded by the Arabic-Islamic contribution, culminating in al-Fārābi's own massive logical output.[3]

The publication and translation of al-Fārābi's logical works started in the 1950s. It is regrettable, however, that no independent study of that massive contribution has been published in recent years. Ibrahim Madkour's important work *L'Organon d'Aristote au monde Arabe*, published in 1934, does not do justice to the first great Aristotelian logician of Islam for this reason. In fact, Madkour complains in that book that of al-Fārābi's

2. Cf. Kneale, *The Development of Logic*, pp. 198f.
3. Cf. Fakhry, 'Al-Fārābi's Contribution to the Development of Aristotelian Logic', pp. 7–15.

'numerous writings and commentaries on the different parts of the *Organon*, no more than fragmentary and insufficient data have reached us'.[4] For this reason, we are told, that author reluctantly chose al-Fārābi's great disciple and successor, Ibn Sīna, as the representative of the Arabic logical tradition. Ibn Sīna may in fact have outstripped his master in thoroughness, but he remains nonetheless dependent on him in the field of logic, as he was in the fields of cosmology and metaphysics. In the fields of ethics and politics, the contribution of the disciple was insignificant compared with that of the master. Moreover Madkour's statement should be revised now in the light of the discovery, since the 1950s, of al-Fārābi's voluminous logical output.

4. Madkour, *L'Organon d'Aristote*, p. 9.

Appendix

[The following excerpt, from *'Uyūn al-Anbā'*, by the late biographer Ibn Abī Usyabi'ah (d. 1270), includes, in addition to his life, this fragment of al-Fārābi's lost treatise on the *Rise of Philosophy* (*Fi Ẓuhūr al-Falsafah*).]

I

Abū Nasr al-Fārābi is Abū Naṣr Muḥammad Ibn Muḥammad Ibn Uzalāgh Ibn Tarkhān. His birthplace was Fārāb, a city of the land of the Turks in the (Province) of Khurāsan. His father was an army captain of Persian extraction. He dwelt in Baghdad for a while, then moved to Damascus, where he stayed up to his death.

He was, God have mercy on him, a perfect philosopher and a perfect Imām, who mastered the philosophical sciences and excelled in the mathematical sciences. He was pure in heart, superior of intelligence, averse to the world and contented with the necessities of life, following in the footsteps of ancient philosophers. He also had a certain proficiency in the art of medicine and some knowledge of its universal principles, although he never practiced it or sought to learn its particulars.

I was told by Sayf al-Dīn Abū-l-Hasan 'Alī Ibn Abī 'Ali al-Āmidi that al-Fārābi worked at first as a garden-keeper in Damascus, while he continued to engage in the study of philosophy [*hikmah*], investigating it, seeking the opinions of the ancients and explaining its meanings. He was of limited resources, so much so that he spent the night reading and writing by the light of the night-watchman. He continued in that state for a while; then his station improved and his merit became known to the public. His writings became famous and his students grew in number, until he was recognized as the unique (philosopher) and the most learned scholar of his time.

He met Sayf al-Dawlah, Abū'l-Hasan 'Ali Ibn 'Abdullah Ibn Hamdān of the Taghlib tribe, who honored him vastly and his position grew in his eyes. He was his favorite.

I have copied from the hand of some old masters that Abū Naṣr al-Fārābi traveled to Egypt in the year 338 H. [AD 949 CE] and then returned to Damascus, where he died in the month of Rajab, 339 H. [950 CE] at the court of Sayf al-Dawlah, during the caliphate of al-Rāḍi. Sayf al-Dawlah performed the ritual prayer at the head of fifteen members of his choice courtiers.

It is said that he did not receive from Sayf al-Dawlah, in addition to what he favored him with, more than four silver dirhams a day, which he spent on the purchase of the necessities of life. He did not pay attention to his looks, his home or his means of livelihood.

It is said that he used to feed on the juice of the hearts of lambs, together with Rayhani wine only. It is also said that, early in his life, he served as a judge, but when he discovered the merit of (philosophical) learning, he abandoned that and bent all his efforts on acquiring it. He never settled down to any worldly occupation.

It is said that he used to go out at night from his home to read by the watchmen's torch. He attained in the theory and practice of music, which he mastered, the highest degree. It is said that he constructed once a strange (musical) instrument, which produced magnificent sounds which could move the emotions.

It is said that the reason why he engaged in reading philosophy books is that someone left a collection of Aristotle's books in his care. He happened to look into them and like them. He thus proceeded to reading them and continued to do so until he mastered their intent and became a true philosopher.

I have copied some words of Abū Naṣr on the meaning of the term philosophy. He wrote: 'The name of philosophy comes from Greek and is a borrowed word in Arabic, which in their tongue is *filusufia*, meaning the love of wisdom. It is compounded in their tongue of *fila*[1] and *sufia*; *fila* meaning 'love' and *sufia* meaning 'wisdom'. The term 'philosopher' derives from that of 'philosophy', which in their language is '*philo-sophos*'. This is a common form of derivation in their language. It means a lover of wisdom; being, according to him, one who devotes his entire life to the search for wisdom.

II

Abū Naṣr al-Fārābi relates in *The Rise of Philosophy* the following, which I give verbatim: 'Philosophy flourished for the first time, during the reign of the Greek kings. Following the death of Aristotle [i.e. 322 BCE], it gained ground at Alexandria up to the last days of the Woman [i.e. Cleopatra, d. 39 BCE]. Instruction [*ta'lim*] continued following his death[2] unchanged, until thirteen (Ptolemaic) kings succeeded each other. During that period, twelve teachers of philosophy flourished, one of whom was named Andronicus (of Rhodes) [fl. *c.* 40 CE]. The last of the (Ptolemaic) rulers was the Woman [i.e. Cleopatra], who was defeated by Augustus, the King [Emperor] of Rome. He killed her and seized the throne. When he felt secure, he looked into the book-collections and classified them. He found therein copies of Aristotle's writings, compiled during his days or those of Theophrastus [d. 288 BCE].[3] He, also, found that teachers and philosophers had written other books, dealing with the same subjects Aristotle had dealt with. He [i.e. Augustus] ordered that these books, compiled in Aristotle's days and those of his pupils, be copied and serve as the basis of instruction, and the rest to be discarded.

He [Augustus] entrusted this task to Andronicus and ordered him to make some copies, which he could carry with him to Rome, and others that could be kept in the 'Center of Instruction'.[4] He also ordered him to appoint a teacher to fill his position in Alexandria, and to accompany him

1. Or rather, *filu* (*philo*).
2. That is, Aristotle's.
3. Immediate successor of Aristotle as head of the Lyceum.
4. Or School of Alexandria.

[i.e. the Emperor] to Rome. Thus, there were two centers of learning at that time and this continued until the rise of Christianity. Thereupon, instruction in Rome stopped, but continued in Alexandria until such time as the Christian king [kings?] had time to look into this matter.

The bishops met and conferred as to what should be retained of that instruction and what should be dropped. They decided that of the logical works [of Aristotle, i.e. the *Organon*], students should be taught up to the end of the 'existential moods' (of the syllogism),[5] but not beyond, because they thought that would constitute a threat to Christianity. It was felt that what was authorized could be used in support of their religion. Thus, the public part of instruction (in logic) remained unchanged, while the rest was kept hidden until the advent of Islam a long time after. Thereupon, instruction was moved from Alexandria to Antioch, where it continued for a long time, until one teacher was left. Two men studied with him, one from the inhabitants of Harrān, the other of Merw. They left, carrying the books with them.

As for the man from Merw, he had two students, Ibrāhim al-Marwazi and Yuḥannā Ibn Ḥaylān. From the Harrānean, Isrā'īl the Bishop and Quwayri received instruction. The two moved to Baghdad where Ibrāhim engaged in religious activity, while Quwayri took up teaching. As for Yuḥannā Ibn Ḥaylān, he, too, engaged in religious activity; while Ibrāhim al-Marwazi then moved to Baghdad, where he settled down. Mattā Ibn Yunān[6] received instruction from al-Marwazi. Instruction at that time ended with the 'existential moods' of the syllogism.

Abū Naṣr al-Fārābi himself reports that he received instruction from Yuḥanna Ibn Ḥaylān up to the end of *Analytica Posteriora* (*Kitāb al-Burhān*). What came after the 'existential moods' used to be called the unread part, until it was read then. The rule, thereafter, once the responsibility devolved upon Muslim teachers, was to read what one was able to read of the existential moods. Abū Nasr states that he read up to the end of *Analytica Posteriora* [*Kitāb al-Burhān*].[7]

5. That is, the categorical moods discussed in Book I of *Analytica Priora*. That curriculum included the *Categories*, *De interpretatione*, Book I of the *Analytica Priora*, and the *Isagoge* of Porphyry. These were known as the 'four books', and excluded the *Analytica Posteriora* (*Kitāb al-Burhān*), mentioned later in the Ibn Abī 'Usaybi'ah excerpt.
6. Also known as Ibn Yunus.
7. This sounds like a repetition.

My uncle, Rashīd al-Dīn Abū'l-Hasan 'Ali Ibn Khalīfah, may his soul rest in peace, told me that al-Fārābi died at the court of Sayf al-Dawlah Ibn Hamdān in the month of Rajab of the Year 339 H. [950 CE]. He learned the art (of logic) from Yuḥannā Ibn Ḥaylān in Baghdad, during the reign of the Abbassid Caliph, al-Muqtadir. Abū al-Mubashshir[8] Mattā Ibn Yunān was his contemporary; he was older than Abū Naṣr, but Abū Naṣr was more acute and better spoken.

(Taken from Ibn Abī Usaybi'ah, *'Uyūn al-Anbā'*, pp. 603–605.)

8. Usually known as Abū Bishr.

Bibliography

Al-Fārābi's writings

Al-Alfāz al-Musta'malah fi'l-Mantiq, ed. M. Mahdi, Beirut, 1968.

Arā' Ahl al-Madīnah al-Fādilah, ed. A. Nader, Beirut, 1959.

Falsafat Aflātun, ed. F. Rosenthal and R. Walzer, London, 1973.

Falsafat Aristutālīs, ed. M. Mahdi, Beirut, 1961.

Fī Ithbāt al-Mufāriqat, Hyderabad, 1926.

Fuṣūl Muntaza'ah, ed. F. Najjar, Beirut, 1971.

Al-Fuṣūl al-Khamsah, ed. D.M. Dunlop, *Islamic Quarterly*, 2, 1955, pp. 264–74.

Iḥṣā' al-'Ulūm, ed. U. Amin, Cairo, 1968.

Introductory Risālahon Logic, ed. D.M. Dunlop, *Islamic Quarterly*, 2, 1955, pp. 224–74.

Introductory Sections on Logic, ed. D.M. Dunlop, *Islamic Quarterly*, 2, 1955, pp. 264–74.

Isāghugi, ay al-Madkhal, ed. D.M. Dunlop, *Islamic Quarterly*, 3, 1956, pp. 117–27.

Al-Jam' Bayn Ra'yay al-Hakīmayn, ed. A. Nader, Beirut, 1960.

Jawāmi' al-Shi'r (*Appendix Talkhīs Kitāb Arisṭuṭālis fi'l-Shi'r li Ibn Rushd*), ed. M.S. Salim, Cairo, 1971.

Kitāb al-Burhān, ed. M. Fakhry, Beirut, 1987.

Kitāb al-Hurūf, ed. M. Mahdi, Beirut, 1970.

Kitāb al-Khatābāh, in *Deux ouvrages inédits sur la rhetorique*, ed. J. Langhade and M. Grignaschi, Beirut, 1971.

Kitāb al-Millah wa Nuṣūs Ukhra, ed. M. Mahdi, Beirut, 1968.

Kitāb al-Musīqa al-Kabīr, ed. Gh. A-M. Khashabah and M.A. al-Hanafi, Cairo, 1967.

Kitāb Qātiguriās, ay al-Madkhal, ed. D.M. Dunlop, *Islamic Quarterly*, 4, 1957, pp. 168–183.

Kitāb Qātiguriās, ay al-Madkhal (cont'd), ed. D.M. Dunlop, *Islamic Quarterly*, 5, 1959, pp. 21–37.

Risālah fi'l-'Aql, ed. M. Bouyges, Beirut, 1938.

Risālah fi'l-Tawti'ah, ed. D.M. Dunlop, *Islamic Quarterly*, 3, 1955, pp. 224–35.

Sharh Kitāb al-'Ibārah, ed. W. Kutsch and S. Marrow, Beirut, 1960.

Al-Siyāsah al-Madaniyah, ed. F. Najjar, Beirut, 1964.

Tahsīl al-Sa'ādah, ed. Ja'far Āl Yasin, Beirut, 1983.

Talkhīs Nawāmis Aflātun, ed. F. Gabrieli, London: Warburg Institute, 1952.

Al-Tanbīh 'alā Sabīl al-Sa'ādah, ed. J. Āl Yasin, Beirut, 1987.

Al-Thamarh al-Mardiyah fi Ba'd al-Risālat al-Fārābiyah, ed. F. Dieterici, Leiden, 1890. (Cf. translations.) Includes: *Al-Jam' Bayna Ra'yay al-Hakīmayn*; *Fī Aghrād al-Hakīm*; *Fī Ma'āni al-'Aql*; *Fī Mā Yanbaghi an Yuqaddam Qabl Ta'allum al-Falsafah*; *'Uyūn al-Masā'il*; *Fusūs al-Hikam*; *Fī Jawāb Masā'il Su'ila 'Anhā*; *Fī Mā Yaṣuḥḥ wa Mā lā Yaṣuḥḥ min 'Ilm Aḥkām al-Nujūm*.

Translations

Butterworth, Charles E. *Alfarabi, the Political Writings: Selected Aphorisms and Other Texts*, Ithaca and London: Cornell University Press, 2001.

Dieterici, F. *Al-Fārābi's Philosophische Abhandlungen*, Leiden: E.J. Brill, 1892 (reprinted Frankfurt: Minerva, 1976). (Cf. *al-Thamarah al-Mardiyah, Arabic Writings*.)

Dunlop, D.M., *Al-Fārābi's Eisagoge*, *Islamic Quarterly*, 3, 1956, pp. 117–38.

—— *Introductory 'Risālah' on Logic*, *Islamic Quarterly*, 2, 1955, pp. 230–35.

—— *Introductory Sections on Logic*, *Islamic Quarterly*, 2, 1955, pp. 274–82.

—— *Paraphrase of the 'Categories' of Aristotle*, *Islamic Quarterly*, 4, 1957, pp. 183–197.

—— *Paraphrase of the 'Categories' of Aristotle (cont'd), Islamic Quarterly*, 5, 1959, pp. 37–54.

Hyman, A. 'The Letter Concerning the Intellect', in *Philosophy in the Middle Ages*, ed. A. Hyman and J. Walsh, Indianapolis: Hacket, 1987.

Mahdi, M. *The Philosophy of Plato and Aristotle*, New York: Glencoe Press, 1962. Includes the *Attainment of Happiness.*

Najjar, F. and Mallet, D. *L'harmonie entre les opinions de Platon et d'Aristote*, Damascus: Institute Français de Damas, 1999 (with Arabic text).

Palencia, A.G. *Catalogo de los Ciencias*, Madrid: Institu Miguel Asin, 1953.

Walzer, R. *Al-Fārābi on the Perfect State*, Oxford: Clarendon Press, 1985.

Zimmerman, F.W. *Al-Fārābi's Commentary and Short Treatise on Aristotle's De interpretatione*, London: Oxford University Press, 1981.

Arabic sources and references

Al-Ghazāli, A.H. *Tahāfut al-Falāsifah*, ed. M. Bouyges, Beirut, 1927.

Gohlman, W.E. *Life of Ibn Sīna* (Arabic text), New York, 1974.

Ibn Abī Usaybi'ah, A. *'Uyūn al-Anbā'*, ed. N. Rida, Beirut, 1965.

Ibn Bājjah, A.B. *Opera Metaphysica*, ed. M. Fakhry, Beirut, 1968.

—— *Ta'āliq 'ala Mantiq al-Fārābi*, ed. M. Fakhry, Beirut, 1994.

Ibn Khallikān. *Wafayāt al-A'yān*, Cairo, 1948.

Ibn Maynūn, M. *Dalālat al-Hā'irin*, ed. H. Atai, Cairo, 1980.

Ibn al-Nadīm. *Kitāb al-Fihrist*, Cairo, no date.

Ibn Rushd (Averroes), A.W. *Fasl al-Maqāl*, ed. A. Nader, Beirut, 1961.

—— *al-Kashf 'an Manāhij al-Adillah*, ed. M. Qasim, Cairo, 1961.

—— *Tahāfut al-Tahāfut*, ed. M. Bouyges, Beirut, 1930.

—— *Talkhīs al-Khatābah*, ed. A-R. Badawi, Cairo, 1960.

—— *Talkhīs al-Qiyās*, ed. M. Qasim, Cairo, 1987.

—— *Talkhīs Kitāb al-Maqūlat*, ed. M. Qasim, Cairo, 1980.

—— *Talkhīs Kitāb Aristutālis fi'l-Shi'r*, ed. M.S. Salim, Cairo, 1971.

Al-Kindi, A.Y. *Rasā'il al-Kindi al-Falsafiyah*, ed. A. Abū Rida, Cairo, 1950.

Khalifah, Hajji *Kash al-Zunūn*, Leipzig and London, 1835–58.

Al-Māwardi. *Al-Aḥkām al-Ṣulṭāniyah*, Beirut, 1985.

Al-Qifti. *Tarīkh Al-Hukamā'*, ed. J. Lippert, 1903.

Al-Suhrawardi, Sh.-D. *Oeuvres Philosophiques et Mystiques*, ed. H. Corbin, Tehran and Paris, 1952.

Sā'id, Ibn Sā'id (al-Andalusi). *Tabaqāt al-Uman*, ed. L. Sheikho, Beirut, 1912.

Al-Tawhidi, A.H. *Al-Imtā' wa'l-Mu'ānassah*, ed. A. Amin and A. al-Zayn, Beirut, 1953.

Works in Western Languages

Abed, Shukri. Aristotelian Logic and the Arabic Language in Al-Fārābi, Albany: SUNY Press, 1991.

Aquinas, St. Thomas. *Basic Writings*, ed. A. Pegis, New York: Random House, 1945.

Aristotle. *Basic Works*, ed. R. McKeon, New York: Randon House, 1941.

Bédoret, H. 'Les premières traductions Tolédanes de philosophy; Oeuvres d'Al-Farabi', Revue Néoscolastique de Philosophie, 41, 1938, pp. 80–96.

Fakhry, M. 'Al-Fārābi and the Reconciliation of Plato and Aristotle', Journal of the History of Ideas, 26, 1965, pp. 469–78.

—— *A History of Islamic Philosophy*, New York: Columbia University Press, 1983.

—— 'The Ontological Argument in the Arabic Tradition: The Care of al-Fārābi', *Studia Islamica*, 64, 1986, pp. 5–17.

—— 'Al-Fārābi's Contribution to the Development of Aristotelian Logic', in *Philosophy, Dogma and the Impact of Greek Thought*, III, Aldershot: Ashgate, 1994, pp. 7–15.

Farmer, H.G. *A History of Arabian Music*, London: Luzac, 1973.

Gohlman, W.E. *Life of Ibn Sīna* (Arabic text), Albany: SUNY Press, 1974.

Kneale, W. and Kneale M. *The Development of Logic*, Oxford: Clarendon Press, 1962.

Madkour, I. *La Place d'al-Fārābi dans l'École Philosophique Musulmane*, Paris: Libraire d'Amerique et d'Orient, 1934.

—— *L'Organon d'Aristote au Monde Arabe*, Paris: J. Vrin, 1934.

Maimonides, M. 'Letter to Samuel Ben Tibbon', in *Iggerot ha-Ramban*, rev. edn. ed. Itshak Shailat, Ma'aleh Adumin, Israel: Shailat, 1995.

—— *The Guide of the Perplexed*, trans. S. Pines, Chicago: University of Chicago Press, 1963.

Netton, I.R. *Al-Fārābi and His School*, London and New York: Routledge, 1992.

Plato. *The Collected Works*, ed. E. Hamilton and H. Cairns, Princeton: Princeton University Press, 1961.

Rescher, N. *Al-Fārābi, an Annotated Bibliography*, Pittsburgh: Pittsburgh University Press, 1962.

—— 'Al-Farabi on Logical Tradition', *Journal of the History of Ideas*, 24, 1963, pp. 127ff.

—— *The Development of Arabic Logic*, Pittsburgh: Pittsburgh University Press, 1964.

Ross, W.D. *Aristotle*, London: Methuen, 1956.

Salmon, D. 'The Medieval Latin Translations of Alfarabi's Works', New Scholasticism, 13, 1939, pp. 245–61.

Shehadi, F. *Philosophies of Music in Medieval Islam*, Leiden: E.J. Brill, 1995.

Stenschneider, M. *Al-Fārābi, Leben und Schriften*, St. Petersburg: Academy of Sciences, 1889 (reprinted Amsterdam: Philo Press 1996).

Windelband, M. *History of Ancient Philosophy*, trans. H.E. Cushman, New York: Dover, 1956.

Wright, W. *History of Syriac Literature*, London, 1894.

Index

Lightning Source UK Ltd.
Milton Keynes UK
UKOW03f0655260314

228836UK00002B/20/P

9 781851 683024